Praise for *Everything a New Elementary School Teacher REALLY Needs to Know*

"Good advice for novice and veteran teachers alike. Whether readers take in the guide from cover to cover or dip in as needed (which will be often), they will leave with a greater sense of confidence."

—ForeWord

"This book is a treasure trove of 'for real' tasty tidbits of advice. Kriegel writes well enough to read it through like a novel, but there is so much useful information I have placed it in a handy location, so when a question comes up or a school routine looms ominously in the near future, I can go to the table of contents and use the book like a good old-fashioned Farmers' Almanac."

—Jon Snyder, Dean of the Bank Street College of Education

"Otis Kriegel is the teacher every parent wants their child to have. For those who care about improving the quality of our schools you simply have to hope that elementary teachers and parents will buy and read this book."

—Bob Kerrey, president emeritus, The New School

"When I first started teaching, I didn't even know what I didn't know. I couldn't figure out why it felt like my students were running the class. How I wish I'd had Otis Kriegel's book back then! This is an indispensable guide for any teacher, whether they're just starting out or looking for straight-up, sensible advice on how to improve their classroom and their practice."

—Dan Moulthrop, coauthor, with Dave Eggers and Ninive Calegari, of *Teachers Have It Easy: The Big Sacrifices and Small Salaries of America's Teachers*

"A terrific guide filled with excellent tips and suggestions for new teachers."

—Steve Reifman, National Board Certified Teacher and author of *Eight Essentials for Empowered Teaching and Learning, K–8*

"Drawing upon his own years of teaching and reflections on what it means to teach well, Kriegel offers readers a practical, personable road map for how they can become better teachers."

—Brad Olsen, associate professor of education, University of California, Santa Cruz, and author of *Teaching What They Learn, Learning What They Live: How Teachers' Personal Histories Shape Their Professional Development*

"Kriegel's the hurricane of fresh air that elementary teacher education needs today."

—Joseph Patrick Rafter, Ph.D, clinical assistant professor, Steinhardt School of Culture, Education, and Human Development, New York University

"Sweeping and practical guidance to the novice teacher. Through engaging anecdote and lucid reflection, Kriegel draws on his own professional journey in making a vital contribution to the field of teacher education."

—Michael Grady, Ed.D., deputy director and clinical assistant professor, Annenberg Institute for School Reform at Brown University

"A delightful book, chock-full of practical advice for new teachers. Where else will you learn to keep a change of clothes handy (in case a child pees on you) or to tell a parent volunteer that the snacks are for the CHILDREN (and that she shouldn't eat them all herself)?"

—Clara Hemphill, founding editor of InsideSchools.org and author of *New York City's Best Public Elementary Schools*

"In these pages teachers will find ways to mend the disconnect they commonly feel between their reasons for choosing teaching and the fears about struggles in the early part of their careers. Covering crucial territory that is often overlooked in certification programs, . . . Kriegel guides the reader with humor, care, and incisive intelligence. It's a book to devour from cover to cover, and to return to often."

—Andra Miletta, assistant professor, Mercy College

"Finally, a practical survival guide for first-year teachers that provides the blueprint for what you need to do—and how—to be an effective teacher. Every teacher beginning their career should have this book."

—Andrea Franks, veteran 4th- and 5th-grade teacher, New York City

"Otis Kriegel has provided sound, pragmatic advice on the multitude of topics and issues that brand-new teachers brave in their first year. School administrators should enclose a copy of this book with every signed contract. Many teachers leave the profession within the first five years of teaching because they are overwhelmed by the vast responsibilities of the job. We administrators are challenged to find genuine, meaningful ways to support them. Kriegel taps into his substantial teaching experience to weave together a comprehensive roadmap to student success and support, coupled with increased teacher satisfaction and competence."

—Lois Kortum, 40-year veteran independent school administrator

Everything a New Elementary School Teacher REALLY Needs to Know

(But Didn't Learn in College)

Otis Kriegel, M.S.Ed.

free spirit
PUBLISHING®

Every chapter is chock full of advice, tips, and guidelines that you can take as is or tweak to fit your own needs. You'll also find true stories—anecdotes I experienced or heard from friends (they're printed in **this font**). Boxed sections labeled BTW ("By the Way") are little tidbits of information or quick tips that you may find important.

You're lucky. As a teacher, you're not going to be stuck behind a desk all day, and you *definitely* won't be bored! You're on the front line of society, working hand in hand with the future leaders of the towns, cities, and countries that make up our planet. It's inspiring, energizing, humbling, and incredibly rewarding work.

Get in there, be proud, and have fun.

OTIS KRIEGER

P.S. I would love to hear how this book has helped you in your first years of teaching. If you have any stories or questions for me, I can be reached through my publisher at:

Free Spirit Publishing Inc.
6325 Sandburg Road, Suite 100
Golden Valley, MN 55427-3674
www.freespirit.com
help4kids@freespirit.com

BEFORE THE SCHOOL YEAR

Picture this: You open the door to your new classroom on a sunny morning in August. You see stacks of dusty tables and chairs, a teacher's desk stuck between a few empty bookshelves, and maybe a few dictionaries and math books. Stubs of pencils and paperclips have been swept into a corner along with broken pieces of chalk—even though you don't have a chalkboard in the room.

Or maybe the room you walk into is clean but empty, or maybe the walls and bulletin boards are still plastered with student work and visual aids from the class that occupied the room last year.

Whatever state you find your new classroom in, it may be hard to imagine what it will look like with 30 kids and you, all working in harmony. You may think, "I'm supposed to change this into a learning environment? Is this a joke?"

Take a deep breath. With a little time and preparation, you—and your class—will be fine.

In this section, you'll learn how to turn a mess—or a sterile room—into a friendly, efficient learning environment. You'll also learn how to soak up the school culture, practices, and expectations on the fly.

The most important thing to remember is that every situation is different for a new teacher. Use what applies to your circumstances. Feel free to make adjustments. Read on for ideas to make your classroom, and your role in the school culture, fit who you are.

Chapter

ONE

Making Your Classroom Work for You

It can be reassuring to look into the classroom and imagine 30 students hustling their way through the day, thinking, talking, and exploring. But before the classroom is set up, that image can seem as far away as a tropical island when you're standing in the middle of a hailstorm. To get everything organized the way you want, give yourself at least three to four days.

What does a terrific teacher's classroom look like? It can be the essence of organization, or it can look, to an outsider at least, like a mass of chaos and confusion. Some teachers put desks in rows and others group tables together. Some have massive, ocean-sized rugs where they do the majority of their teaching, while others use a mix of different styles. On your way to becoming that terrific teacher, you'll have many decisions to make about desks, rugs, supply shelves, decorations, and a lot more. As you work through all these details, your style will begin to emerge. But be open to changing as the year progresses.

Use the ideas in this chapter as inspiration and a guide, adjusting what you need to make the classroom work for you.

ROOM DESIGN AND TRAFFIC PATTERNS

When setting up desks, tables, chairs, bookshelves, the classroom library, learning centers, cubbies, and bulletin boards, the most important factor to consider is traffic. You and your students will be moving around this room all day. You need to be able to get from one side of the room to the other without causing a minor catastrophe like tripping over a student's lunch box, backpack, or foot.

Also, you should be able to see everyone from anywhere. It's nice to have a little library nook in a first-grade class, filled with bean bags and pillows, but if you can't see in there, who knows what's happening? You need to be able to stand up and look across the room and see what's going on in each and every corner. What you can't see is what you don't know, and what you don't know may very well spell trouble.

> I thought I had set up such a nice first-grade classroom. There were little learning nooks, well-organized learning centers, and assigned desks for group work. I was working in a corner of the room at a kidney-shaped table with a small group of students when I heard one of my students yell at another. I looked out across the room but couldn't see who it was. I stood, and I could just see the tops of their heads as they wrestled in the library area. By the time I got to them—after tripping over a desk and knocking over a box of crayons—they were both crying and angry. If I had thought of the importance of being able to easily travel across the room, I could have avoided having to jump over various pieces of furniture to break up the skirmish. And if I could have seen what was happening I could have intervened sooner.

Before you begin to organize your desks (or tables if you'll be using them instead), try to find out how many you're going to need. Get your class list or at least an estimate of how many kids will be in your class.

Next, think about how you want to group your desks. Many elementary school teachers put desks or tables together in clusters so students sit in groups of two to six, while others prefer rows. I like clusters because it helps kids naturally learn from each other, not just me, and they can easily work together in groups or independently as the situation calls for. The downside of clusters is that it can promote student chatter. Rows can keep the class quieter, but I think rows are isolating for students. Besides, nowhere else in life will they sit in rows except when taking their drivers' test at the DMV.

Your school may have a preference, and you can also get ideas from looking at other classrooms in your school and talking to other teachers.

BTW: It can be fun to name clusters or tables after a part of the curriculum. If you're studying the state in which you teach, name them after important locations or events. For example, when I taught first grade, we were studying the neighborhood, so I named the tables after local street names. When my students went outside after school, they recognized the street signs as the same words used at their table. I heard, "Hey, I know what that says! I can read that!"

Once you have some ideas, decide on a plan and set up your desks. Then pull out the chairs just slightly from the desks to emulate how they'll be with kids sitting and working. Walk through the room. Can you make it from one side to the other without tripping? Do you need to crawl over a desk? If so, change the design until you can get across the room easily from multiple starting points. Take the time to try several setups. You might want to make drawings so you can check out a few different plans quickly.

After you've set up your desks or tables, leave them alone for a day and begin to work on other parts of the floor plan, like the meeting area, the library, and the shelves that will hold supplies. As the rest

of the room takes shape, you may notice congestion or other problems you hadn't thought of before. Remember: you can always change your classroom setup. It's not set in stone or bolted to the floor. (At least I hope it isn't!)

Never block the door or put a student's desk near the door. The student sitting there will get no work done at all because she'll be distracted by students and adults coming and going. You're also going to need fresh air in the classroom, so be sure not to block the windows either (if you have them). You want to be able to easily open and close them.

> **BTW:** If you can, squeeze in a place in the classroom for one table or desk away from the others. This can be called the "Alone Table." Use it as a place to send kids who are distracting others or for someone who needs some time away from the group to calm down or concentrate. The Alone Table will come in handy on an almost daily basis. If you don't have an extra table, use a pillow and a clipboard.

Finally, remember that a warm classroom can put kids to sleep. I like to keep my classroom temperature brisk yet comfortable, so students are aware and awake. If you work in a consistently warm area of the country, purchase a number of small fans to keep the air circulating. And remember, kids can get smelly. Airflow throughout the classroom keeps things smelling better and naturally cleans out germs. And you'll have plenty of those!

Two Designs for Smooth Traffic Flow

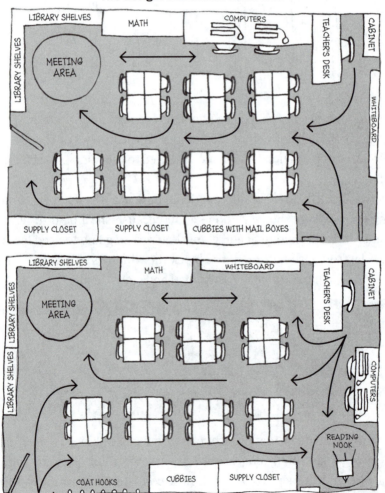

THE TEACHER'S DESK

"I haven't sat at my desk for a week," one veteran teacher complained to me. "I'm getting rid of it. It doesn't make sense to keep it."

It's your choice whether to have a teacher's desk, so think about how you'll use it. If it's just going to end up being a large piece of furniture taking up space, ditch it. Instead of a desk, I use a small table next to two file cabinets in the corner of the room. This is where I put things like papers to file, papers to grade, pens, and others things that are important to me in the near future (within the next few days). My setup wasn't always like this.

During my first year of teaching I had a real "teacher's desk." I never taught from it, but it was a very prominent part of the classroom. One afternoon my students were working on group projects. All of the tables in the room were occupied, and two students had nowhere to work. I suggested they work on the rug, but neither of them wanted to. They had spent the better part of the morning on the rug. One of the two students was very tall (for a second grader) and wanted to sit up. His back hurt from bending over on the rug. We looked around and couldn't find a spot. Finally, one of the kids looked at my desk, which was covered in papers, curriculum guides, and pencils. "Why can't we use your desk?" she asked. My first thought was "No way. That's *my* desk." But I quickly realized it was a great idea. The desk was taking up a lot of room. "We'll even clean it up for you, Mr. K," she continued, "because it's really messy." Together we cleaned it off and, to my surprise and their amusement, we recycled half of the paperwork. That afternoon I got rid of the desk and replaced it with a smaller table that was more kid-friendly as well as two portable plastic file boxes that I still have. When my students arrived the next morning, the two who had worked at my desk noticed the change. One commented, "Good job." The other, who had a critical eye and a

more judgmental tone, was more direct: "That desk was stupid. It was too big and messy and you were never there, anyway. You're always with us." They were both right.

I've seen teachers position a desk front and center and teach from it. Personally, I don't find that effective. I cannot manage a class or teach effectively from the seat of my pants. I want to be up and moving around. Still, there are some very creative ways to effectively use a desk in the classroom. A friend of mine puts his desk in the middle of the classroom and decorates it with bins and shelves on three sides. This is where students leave finished work or grab new work while he conferences with other students, makes edits, records progress, and restocks bins with different assignments.

Instead of a desk, one teacher I know uses 10 to 15 file folders stapled to a cork or foam board. Each folder is labeled with the name of an academic subject or other topic such as "Parent Correspondence," and she files her papers into them right there on the wall. As she says, "It keeps me organized and doesn't take up floor space."

My mother did her student teaching with a woman who'd worked with legendary education reformer John Dewey. This woman didn't believe in using a desk. Instead, she wore it! Every day she dressed in overalls and kept supplies that she needed, like a stapler, pencils, erasers, sharpeners, crayons, markers, and more, on her body. She was like a moving office supply store. If you needed it, she had it.

Again, it's your choice if you want to use a desk. A desk can be a convenient place to store your supplies and personal items. It can also inhibit a friendly classroom tone, take up a lot of room, and end up collecting a lot of junk. The right answer is what works well for you and your teaching style. Think it over and experiment, but keep in mind that space for the kids is the priority. If you do use a teacher's desk, try not to spend too much time sitting there or it can reduce interaction with students. If you find yourself presiding over class from the desk too often, it's time to get off your backside and get to work!

THE MEETING AREA

The meeting area is often considered a hub of a classroom, around which all activity centers. So where does the almighty meeting area go? It depends upon the size and shape of your room, of course, and you might not have space for it. If you do, the most important factor is to make sure you have enough space for your students to come together without sitting on top of each other. Also, the meeting area must be accessed from multiple places in the room. You might be conducting a meeting or a lesson and someone will arrive late, need to use the restroom, or get picked up early. Students must be able to leave and return without disturbing other students. I learned this from watching another teacher (something I still do regularly; there is always more to learn).

> One of my colleagues is a truly gifted upper-elementary teacher. She is fun, tough, and very creative. The meeting area is the focal point of her classroom. It's large enough for everyone to sit together in a circle so every member of the class, including herself, can be an equal participant. Outside of the meeting area, she has tables, but she doesn't assign spots to students; instead, they can work at tables or in the meeting area. When you enter her room it feels like everyone is part of one big machine. Kids lie on the rug in the meeting area working on clipboards alone or in groups. Students use cubbies to store their personal items; the rest of the classroom is shared space.

Besides the location of your meeting area, you can even go so far as to plan ahead how you want your students to sit when they are there. Do you want them to sit in a circle or in a clump? When I taught first, second, and third grades, I had my students sit in an organized circle, just like my colleague does with her upper-grade class. I was always a part of that circle. In the upper grades, we sat in more of a clump, or clustered group, because students were more independent and responsible. Still, you have to be careful that students don't hide behind each other. Be sure you can see, and make eye contact with, everyone.

BTW: Set up your meeting area so you can always see the classroom door. That way, you can welcome visitors without having to move or reorient yourself. Whether it's a parent, a superintendent, an observer, the principal, or a student, you want to see who is coming in that door.

Don't be afraid to change from clump to circle or vice versa if one method is not working. If your kids are not paying attention when sitting in a clump, switch to the circle. And if you feel your class can handle the responsibility of breaking the structure of an organized circle, then try the clump. Change to what is going to work for your class and for you.

Another thing you'll need to decide is whether to use a rug. A rug is more comfortable than the floor, but it must be cleaned or little insects—like lice—will live there. You can get a rug and remove it later if it doesn't work for you. If you decide to use a rug in your meeting area, make sure to buy a vacuum or chip in with other teachers on your floor or grade level and share it. Use it daily and wash the carpet every month or so. A rug can get seriously nasty in a hurry.

Don't spend a lot of money on your rug, either. Many teacher supply stores offer rugs with the states or letters on them. If you have the budget, go ahead and get one. Otherwise, go to a local carpet store and tell them you're a teacher and the size you need. If they have a remnant in good shape, they'll likely let you have it. You'd be surprised how willing folks will be to help out a local teacher.

SO MANY SUPPLIES AND SO LITTLE ROOM

You'll have a lot of school supplies, even on the first day, including things like paper, notebooks, folders, pencils, pencil boxes, tape, glue, crayons, and so on. If the school provides supplies, find a place to store them before the students arrive—a place that's easily accessible.

If students are bringing their own school supplies, the first day can be hectic as your empty classroom fills up in a hurry. You can have students put their materials away in their desks or cubbies, but plan to spend a few minutes on this, especially with students in lower elementary classes. If you plan to have all students contribute to a shared collection of school supplies that you will hand out during the year as needed, put out two or three empty crates or boxes and tell students to put their supplies in them. After everyone has arrived, slide the boxes out of the way and deal with them later. Otherwise, you won't be teaching. You'll just be organizing paper, pencils, and markers while simultaneously trying to get to know your new class of students. This is not a good way to begin. But of course, this is a good problem to have. In some situations, you'll receive few supplies at all. If you work in a community where some families can't afford supplies, buy extra if you can afford it and have them on hand.

Backpacks and Jackets

Where are students going to hang their backpacks? Hanging them on the back of chairs can work, but that can impair everyone's ability to move around the room (and ruin your thoughtful classroom traffic plan). If you have a closet with hooks inside, that works great. Hooks on the wall, usually

BTW: If you don't have room elsewhere for jackets, have kids fold them and put them in their backpacks. They only use them a few times a day, and it may save you a lot of space and headaches.

right near the door, work well, too. Some rooms have lockers or cubbies in back, which also work great. In any case, be sure to label the hooks when you get your roster.

Jackets can usually go with backpacks. One year I had a coat rack in the hallway to keep the jackets out of the classroom. I told the kids not to leave any valuables in their jackets, just in case, but after a few items were stolen we brought the coats into our classroom. I recommend you do the same.

BTW: If you don't get a roster until shortly before school starts, label the hooks randomly with numbers. Before kids come into the class, give them each a number and they can find their hook. Later in the day students can label their hooks with their name. Don't assign a shorter student a hook that is too high. That can start some immediate teasing and discomfort for that kid on the first day of school.

Rain and Snow Wear

One morning it was raining sideways and I wasn't prepared. Kids were coming in drenched, and I had no place set aside for their rain gear and wet things. Students were walking around the classroom in rain boots and wet sneakers. The squeaking noise was driving me up the wall. There were puddles all over the place, and the kids were slipping and falling. Two had gotten bruises, which meant phone calls home at lunch. I felt like I was teaching in a swamp. At first the kids thought it was funny, but by lunch everyone was miserable and the room was gross. I used some old newspapers to clean up.

At lunch I talked to a colleague whose room was dry and organized. I asked her how she did it. "On rainy days, I have the kids remove their rain gear and wet clothes and put them in one area to dry," she told me.

"I bought five towels at a dollar store for next to nothing and lay them on the floor where students can leave their wet shoes and other items. Now they don't sit in class wet or squeak as they walk. I can hear your kids from across the hall—it's driving me crazy!" The next day I bought some towels. I'd rather teach kids in their socks than in wet shoes. Now, even during bad storms, my students are dry and happy.

Keep towels or newsprint handy to spread on the floor when it's rainy so kids can leave their footwear and rain gear there to dry. You can also get a bucket or tall plastic trash can to store wet umbrellas. If you live in a snowy climate, gear like snow pants, boots, gloves, hats, and scarves can be an even bigger hassle because of the space they take up and the snow that melts off them, but the same theory can apply. Designate an area for this gear, and keep towels on hand. By planning ahead, you keep the room cleaner and less cluttered when it rains, and the students get out of their wet boots or shoes.

Lunch Boxes

Find an old milk crate, sturdy cardboard box with cutout handles, or a plastic bin and label it "Lunch Box." Put it by the door. When students enter the classroom, they can take their lunches from their backpacks and place them in the box. After everyone has arrived, slide the box out of the way until lunch. Why tell kids to take lunches out of their backpacks? So they won't rummage through their stuff in the rush to go to lunch. You just put out the class lunch box, they get their lunches, and they're on their way. If you have a lot of kids in your class who bring their lunches in brown bags, be sure the bags are clearly labeled so no one is frantically looking for their lunch, and no one steals a lunch that they know (or hope) is better than their own.

If you go on a field trip on a school bus, take the class Lunch Box labeled with your room number and school name. It will keep kids' lunches more organized and easy to track.

DECORATING

I love seeing other teachers' classrooms the day before school starts. I get to learn from my colleagues and feel the current of excitement that flows throughout the school. Some teachers cover the walls with premade "teacher posters" and charts, while others leave their classrooms pretty bare. Often, teachers of lower elementary classes like to put up "Welcome" decorations early in the year. I'm a firm believer in the minimalist approach. At the beginning of the year, I like to keep my room sparse. In three months your classroom is going to be filled with paintings, charts, and other work your students complete. Some teachers like to do a little of both. If you want to use more premade posters at the beginning of the year, consider replacing them with materials you and your students produce during the year. This encourages creativity and helps create a sense of community and class pride.

BTW: Consider engaging teams of students to decorate the outside of your classroom door with themes to match the season or ones they come up with on their own. They will love the opportunity, and it will dress up what can be a drab hallway. As an alternative to that—or even in addition to it—you can hang a cork board to the outside of your classroom door where you can leave notices if you're gone for the day, extra copies of notes sent home in case a parent comes by to get one, or other messages.

CLASSROOM LIBRARY

The classroom library is an integral part of your room, because students will be pulling books from it for assigned reading, free reading, book reports, and more all year long. As a new teacher, focus on two main things right away: how to gather books for your library and how to organize them.

Getting Books

You walk into your classroom and you see a total of three books, including a dictionary, in your library. What do you do? Don't head to the bookstore and spend your first paycheck. You can get free or super cheap books in many ways.

- Visit the other teachers in your grade level and see who can spare some extra books. Most teachers, especially veterans, keep duplicates or books they don't use anymore.

- Go to the librarian or media specialist (if your school has one) and ask for any extras. Grab anything that is appropriate for your grade level—even books a little too advanced and too simple. You never know what the reading level of some of your students will be.

- Ask your principal if there is any extra money in the budget for books.

- Call or write to publishers to see if they have any titles that they would donate in exchange for product feedback, which can be helpful to both you and the publisher. I called a few smaller publishers my first year of teaching and explained that I was a new teacher and I was trying to improve my classroom library. They were happy to send me three new titles in exchange for student feedback. What a deal! And due to their generosity, they got a lifelong customer out of it as well.
- Ask parents to donate books their kids have already read.
- Check out used book stores and garage sales.
- Join book clubs (Scholastic, Children's Book-of-the-Month Club) to earn points to get free or discounted books.

My first classroom library was a random assortment of books including titles published in the 1950s, picture books discarded from other classrooms, and a handful of family donations. I didn't care. It's better to have some books and replace them as the year goes on instead of starting with none—or spending a bunch of your own money on new books.

If you try all of these ideas, you may be surprised by how quickly your classroom library grows. And make sure to label your books with your name and classroom. Books wander, just like other things in schools.

Organization

There are many ways to organize a classroom library. Look around at other teachers' styles to see what they're doing. Here are some ideas to get you started.

Start by setting up the library into fiction and nonfiction sections. I do this whether I am teaching first grade or fifth. It teaches students the difference between the two types of books, and it's an easy way to help kids narrow down their search for a book.

For early elementary classrooms, I typically separate books into baskets using various categories, such as reading level or subject, and organize them within the basket by author, series, or title. Include some baskets related to what or where you are teaching. For example, if I am teaching in a city I'll have a basket of books about city life. Organize your library in a way that is easy to use and is interesting to your students.

One way to supplement your library is to keep a multileveled, multitopic basket on each of your table groups so kids don't need to go to the library to find a book. This can cut down on social interaction and moving back and forth during reading time. As it becomes necessary, refresh the baskets. Sometimes students can help by picking one or two books to keep in the basket and some new titles to add. This table-basket system can be used for both lower and upper grades.

BTW: For lower grades, don't put out all of your books at once. If you introduce them slowly, two or three baskets at a time, your students will not be overwhelmed and they can actually learn about the different aspects of the library and how it functions. You don't want your library jammed with books on the first day of school. It can feel overwhelming to many kids and you don't want to clobber them with too much information at once. Slowly and gently introduce books to them.

For an upper-elementary library, I keep fiction books shelved in alphabetical order according to title, not author, because many students know the books by name. Biographies, autobiographies, science, world history, American history, geography, and reference books like dictionaries and thesauruses define the nonfiction area. These can be shelved by title or subject on the nonfiction bookshelf or organized into baskets. I also like to have several baskets of books grouped by level, well-known or popular authors, multi-book series, specific subjects, and whatever else seems relevant and helpful to my students.

It may not be practical to keep the books in your small classroom library labeled and organized using the Dewey Decimal System, but it's a good idea to introduce it to your students. Most libraries still use it.

BTW: Do your best to keep the classroom library accessible. Don't put it in a part of the classroom that is not easily reached all day. If a student cannot get to the library because of where you're teaching a mini-lesson, you need to move your location or that of the library. You want kids to independently choose books, but if they can't easily get to the library, those excited, motivated students may decide to skip it.

MANIPULATIVES AND OTHER SUPPLIES

If you want your students to use certain items in the classroom, such as scissors, blocks, tiles, or crayons, make them accessible. Put them on a shelf in an area of the classroom that is easily reached by all students. I like to put crayons, colored pencils, drawing paper, scissors, glue, and other art supplies in one area that is near writing supplies such as paper, pencils, reading logs, graphic organizers, or sentence strips. Why? Because they are often used together, so it makes for one trip to one area of the classroom. When I taught first grade I put all of these supplies on a two-sided shelf in the middle of the room, with clusters of desks on opposite sides, so a few students could get the needed material at once without creating a traffic jam.

The most commonly used manipulatives are for math, such as multicolored tiles and Unifix Cubes. Designate an area on a shelf for these learning tools, and put only manipulatives in that specific area. Make sure students know that when they remove them from that shelf, they are to use them for math unless you've designated them for free exploration or another activity.

Just like with books in my classroom library, I like to introduce supplies slowly as they will be used. Put out 26 pencils—not one more—for 26 students, and collect them every day. Have the class use one stapler. As students learn how to use it, put out another. Distribute scissors for a project and then collect them. I don't like to leave anything on the shelf until I'm confident students understand how to use it. This is a process of teaching your students about what tools are available and how to use them responsibly. It's one of the ways you grow the classroom together, creating a community that both students and teacher were a part of building. Starting with an empty room and ending with shelves filled with items that every student knows how to use and respects will help make all of the students feel like they helped set up and create the classroom.

BTW: After you introduce the math manipulatives to your class, it's always wise to schedule a good chunk of time for kids to just play with them before you plan to use them for a lesson. Let the students explore what the manipulatives feel like, build things, and have some unstructured fun. They'll love it! By the time you want your students to use the math manipulatives for math, they aren't being exposed to some brand-new toy and are less likely to play around with them or misuse them.

I was mentoring a new teacher who complained that her students were destroying the classroom math manipulatives and losing all of the art supplies. I asked how she introduced all of these items to her students. "Everything was out on the shelf," she said. I suggested that she remove everything and start over by introducing each item, one by one, down to how to use a pencil sharpener or crayon. She sighed and started to cry, saying, "I feel like I started my year wrong and there is no going back." I reassured her and told her to try it. We removed everything and the next day she reintroduced three items. I checked in with her the following week, after she had reintroduced everything. "They were so sad to see everything off of the shelves, which I felt bad about," she confessed. "But now that we've reviewed how to use each thing, no one is losing anything."

"Not losing anything?" I replied with skepticism.

"Well," she admitted, "a few things—but not as many!"

DON'T FORGET A PADLOCK

Before you leave anything of personal value in your new classroom, make sure you have a safe place for valuables. Your classroom might feature some sort of closet or cabinet that you can lock. If not, find something, like an old locker, that can be secured in your classroom. Just because you lock your classroom door doesn't mean that your keys, phone, wallet, tablet reader, gift card to the local coffee shop, sunglasses, or even laptop are safe. Do you know all of the people who have a key to your room? No. No one does. Lock up your valuables with a padlock. Bring it the first day you go to school, and lock up anything you care about.

Like most teachers I know, I bought a CD player/radio for my classroom. I used it to play the cleanup song (see pages 108–109 in Chapter 4) and to listen to the news as I prepared for the day. The unit cost about $15. It was nothing fancy and it didn't particularly sound good, so it wasn't a big deal to me when it was stolen from my classroom. However, my students, fourth and fifth graders, were outraged. They searched the entire room, accusing me of playing a trick on them. During our Morning Meeting they decided they wanted to write a letter to the thief, explaining how mean they thought it was to steal it. The class separated into small groups, and each collection of students wrote a draft. As a group, we took what we felt were the best sentences and wrote one letter and posted it on the outside of the door. The next morning the stereo reappeared. The kids flipped out. One kid exclaimed, "I knew it was an inside job! Let's dust it for prints and get 'em!" We didn't go that far, but everyone was happy to get our stereo back.

BTW: Don't use a padlock with a key because you can lose that key or someone can take it. Get a combination lock. If you don't have a good memory for those types of things (who does?), write the combination on the bottom of your desk or on a piece of masking tape and stick it underneath the classroom phone. I also create a contact in my cell phone for it. Just name it "Carl Combo" or something like that. That way you'll never lose it.

YOUR LESSON PLAN BOOK

You can choose from a million different types of planning books. Some are vertically organized, some horizontally. Some teachers prefer journals filled with lined paper and some use plain daily calendars. Many teachers like to use electronic planners (such as PlanbookEdu) that allow you to keep your lesson plans and schedules on a laptop, tablet, or even a mobile phone. This can make it easier to share your plans with colleagues.

Find a planner that works for you. If you tend to write a lot of notes every day, you may feel comfortable with a weekly planner with a lot of note space. If you're tech-savvy, you may prefer an electronic version that you can access from your phone as well as your work and home computers. If you prefer to keep it simple, a daily calendar may be more your style. If you go with a physical planner, the inside cover is a great place to keep a list of contact numbers for parents and substitute teachers, along with important dates such as parent-teacher conferences, in-service dates, holidays, birthdays, and upcoming school-wide events.

If you're unsure of what type of lesson plan book you want to use, buy two and use them both the first week of school. Keep the one that works best and give the other to someone who didn't buy one before they were sold out. As with most things mentioned in this chapter, you may start with one type and change to something else later in the year. Be open to making adjustments.

If you're going to buy a more traditional lesson plan book, order it early because they sell out quickly. After all, thousands of other teachers like you are preparing for the first day of school.

STAY COMFORTABLE: CLOTHES AND SHOES

In addition to setting up your classroom, you'll also want to prepare *yourself* for the everyday life of a teacher. That means dressing appropriately. Many teachers' books advise to "dress like a professional" and "never look casual." I think "dressing like a professional" means taking care of yourself. I never look unkempt at work, but since I'm going to be on my feet a lot, I wear footwear that is comfortable. I like to wear dark-colored running shoes, dark-colored sneakers, or boots. Many of my female colleagues leave a pair of flats at school or a dark pair of comfortable shoes. These shoes never come home. This makes life much easier. I walk into my classroom and change shoes. Think of it as preparing for your role.

> **A fellow teacher had a date after school. He decided to stay late at work and go out straight from there. He brought a change of clothes but decided to wear his good shoes to work so he would have them on for the evening. Bad mistake. He stepped in glue, had to break up a fight in the restroom where he stepped in urine, got paint on his shoes when he picked up his class from the art room, and then got blisters from doing recess duty. I went to see him at the end of the day to wish him luck on his date. He was sitting in his classroom looking downright bummed. His dress shoes, once black, sported splashes of purple, green, and yellow. When he saw me he stood up and walked toward me. His shoes made loud sticking noises with every colorful step. It sounded like industrial Velcro being pulled apart. He took them off and started scrubbing them with wet paper towels.**

As an elementary school teacher, you're bound to spend a lot of time sitting on the floor and getting into various messes with kids. Again, you want to look professional, but rethink wearing that fancy new outfit or light-colored pants. I don't recommend you wear paint-flecked old T-shirts and cutoffs, obviously, but clothes that are clean, neat, and attractive don't have to be fancy or expensive.

Your district or school almost certainly has a dress code for teachers, and you should be sure that you adhere to it. You may need to keep religious symbols out of the classroom if you're in a public school, and you may need to keep piercings, tattoos, and undergarments out of view as well.

Be sure to store an extra set of clothes in the room. Teachers ask the families of younger students to send in a change of clothes for kids to keep at school in case of an accident, so why shouldn't teachers do the same? There are five excellent reasons why you should have an extra set of clothes, too. I call them the Five Ps: pee, poo, paint, pens, and puke—not necessarily in that order. (That depends upon your classroom.)

> **Using glitter, glue, and paint, I was doing an art project with my students. We were making Halloween art projects, and one student spilled glue down one leg of my pants. It wasn't a drip, either. I tried my best to wipe it off and return to work when the kid's partner spilled glitter all over the other leg. The kids were laughing their heads off. But I had a change of clothes in my closet so I asked a colleague to watch my class for a matter of moments and returned in clean pants. I wasn't sticky or sparkly anymore—and I stayed a safe distance away from those two students until their cards were done.**

Spare clothes save you from embarrassment, discomfort, and having to spend the afternoon wet or dirty. Put your clothes in a box or bag so they're all in one place and they stay relatively fresh and wrinkle-and-dust free. Stick them in your closet and you'll forget about them until you need them.

SETTING UP FOR THE YEAR, NOT THE MOMENT

If you follow the points in this chapter, you'll avoid a number of hazards that many new teachers experience. From an easy-to-navigate classroom to thoughtful wardrobe decisions, these tips may seem trivial now, but I guarantee they'll pay dividends by helping you feel comfortable and confident when your students arrive.

Chapter

TWO

Learning Your School's Culture

As important as setting up your classroom is getting to know the school you're in. Where do you go for help? What is the recess policy? When do you get observed? What do you do during a fire drill? When is Meet the Teacher Night, and what is required? When is the school building opened in the morning and closed at night?

As much as they're similar, all schools are different. Leadership, teachers, students, parents, staff, neighborhood, and community all help to create an environment that is distinct and original. The resulting way of life—particular to the personalities involved—evolves over time.

This way of life is the school's culture. You'll want to learn as much as you can about it before the first day of school, well before your first student even looks at the front of the building. This chapter will teach you many of the questions to ask and hopefully inspire you to think of others. The answers you get will lead to a smoother start to the school year.

WHO YOU NEED TO KNOW: THE BIG FOUR

Many people play important roles in how a school functions, but four of them are crucial to your success: the office manager (or administrative assistant or secretary), the custodian, the teacher representative (if you have one), and the principal.

The Office Manager, Administrative Assistant, or School Secretary

This person may be known as the head honcho, commandant, or chief, but one thing is almost certainly true: He or she is at the center of all that happens. Keeping an open, friendly, professional relationship with this person will make your school life infinitely smoother. You will most likely visit the office every day, signing in, getting your mail, or asking the office manager questions about a variety of issues, such as sub days, reserving a school bus, a student's permanent record, or the multitude of other issues for which you may need advice. The secretary can help you with the great many administrative needs and questions you will have.

Get to know this key player and try to quickly understand the way things are done in the office. Because schools are awash in a sea of data, paperwork, and legal requirements, probably the most considerate act you can do for the school secretary is to complete and return all the forms and requests with the greatest possible speed. These may not be your top priority, but in the school office they are.

The Custodian

This person manages the infrastructure of the school, doing things like fixing broken doors, leaky windows, and ineffectual heaters, as well as keeping the place clean and safe. The custodian is the in-house handy person, when something breaks or you need help with some physical aspect of your room, he or she is the person to ask. And custodians are usually very busy.

Find out how you can make things easier for the custodian, and the favor will very likely be returned. If the custodian wants you to stack your chairs at the end of the day, train your kids to do it. Find ways to show your appreciation, too. Offer to be the one who takes up a collection during the holidays for the custodian on your floor or wing. Buy a card for your fellow teachers to sign, get everyone to chip in a few bucks, and give it to the custodian before the winter vacation. Gestures like these make a world of difference.

> **I regularly sweep the floor of my classroom, even though I don't need to because the custodian will do it. But I tell him not to sweep. One afternoon, after an especially tough day, there was paint all over the floor, the lock on my door was broken, and I was beat. I was about to head to the hardware store to get some extra cleaning supplies when the custodian came by. "I got it," he said. "Go home. You look exhausted." The next day when I arrived at school, my floor was immaculate, all the whiteboards had been wiped clean, and the lock was fixed. The room looked like new.**

Your Teacher Representative (or Union Representative)

Find out who represents teachers in your school: It may be a union representative or other individual. You may or may not agree with the stances of the organization that represents teachers, but regardless, your teacher rep can provide important information regarding salary steps, in-school elections, and decisions about school-based policies and rallies. Getting to know that person, reading the bulletins, and attending the meetings will help you stay educated on these issues. You will also learn about the politics of education and develop your own stance on issues.

Another good reason to get to know the teacher rep is that she or he can help

BTW: At some schools, you may opt out of representation, and some have different agreements with their employees. Be sure you are very clear about your rights and your responsibilities before you sign on with a school. Make sure you feel comfortable.

protect you if you're investigated or are being treated unfairly by a parent or your administration. The rep can stand between you and potentially unjust or unfair political practices.

> **A colleague of mine was wrongly accused of touching a child inappropriately. The teacher had a stellar record and when the supposed incident took place there were numerous parents present. Nonetheless, she was scared. The child had a record of lying in school and the parents were very unsupportive. My friend notified the representative of the incident and the next day the teacher had a phone call with a union lawyer and an appointment with the school district investigator to move the case along. Instead of dragging out over weeks and months, the union rep's proactive approach helped resolve the conflict quickly.**

The Principal

Although rewarding, the job of principal is also punishing. Principals oversee every aspect of the school, a lot of which involves you and other teachers. They have to cope with a multitude of details daily, and in most cases they can't be on top of everything. It goes without saying that since this is your boss, you will want to do what you can to encourage a mutually respectful relationship.

Chapter 5 has plenty of information about your relationship with your principal, but the most important thing to know is this: Stay in touch with your principal but don't overwhelm him or her. Let the principal know about the terrific things happening in your classroom (it will make her day), be punctual to meetings, and submit paperwork on time. Be respectful of the principal's time. Find out when is the best time to approach the principal with questions so you're more likely to get the answers and help you are looking for.

FINDING A MENTOR

In addition to the Big Four, you'll want to find at least one mentor. It's best to do this before the students arrive or at least in the first month or two of the school year. Many new teachers are assigned mentors, and that can be very helpful, but you may also be saddled with a less-than-helpful mentor. The best mentor is a person you like and respect and who knows his or her way around the school. If you're not assigned to such a person, seek one out.

Think about what type of person you work well with. What are the specifics in which you would like some guidance? Is it curriculum, classroom management, or a combination of the two?

Talk to a few people while they're setting up their classrooms. Ask a few colleagues questions and see which response or attitude you like. Also, ask if there are certain people on staff who have specialties, like incorporating art into the curriculum or math games. Whoever you settle on, it needs to be someone you feel connected to, and, most importantly, trust when asking questions or seeking advice.

> In addition to my assigned mentor my first year, I also found a couple mentors of my own, both in their third year of teaching, which made it easier to relate to them since they were still relatively new. But instead of me simply asking them questions all the time, we decided to occasionally team-teach together. One teamed with me two days per week in the morning for language arts and math, and I teamed up with the other once a week for art and physical education. This was better than peppering them with questions. I was able to learn from watching them teach, and they were able to provide me with pointers when I taught.

Other Important People

The following people can also be great resources for you throughout the year:

- **The math coach, literacy coach, and grade-level leader** are on-site coaches or specialists who can provide you with much needed support as you make your way through the curriculum.

- **The school psychologist** can answer questions you have about a student's IEP (Individualized Education Plan), the document that spells out special services the student receives for special education.

- **The social worker** can answer questions about a child's family history.

- **The guidance counselor** can help when a student needs someone to talk with other than you about problems in or out of the classroom and can provide support when working with a student's family as well.

- **Specialists** help children with specific needs such as reading, speech, and occupational and physical therapy.

- **The technology specialist** is in charge of all of the computers and technology in the building. Find out who this is in case a classroom or resource room computer isn't functioning correctly, you need a special program, or your interactive whiteboard or overhead projector breaks. The specialist also may have extra resources such as tablet computers and ideas for integrating existing devices or your own into your teaching.

It was my first year teaching. I had finished my graduate school courses a month prior, at the end of August, and moved across the country from New York City to Los Angeles to begin my teaching career. In New York, I had become accustomed to school buildings that were three to four stories high rather than spread out on one level, which this one was. I felt disoriented and uncomfortable in my new environment, so I decided to walk the campus, peeking my head into people's classrooms. I introduced myself and explained that I was a new teacher. Naturally, other teachers wanted to know who I was, where I was from, and what grade I was going to teach. By walking around for a few hours I found out about many of the rituals of the school and I also got to know the staff. Through that first walk, I met the two teachers with whom I collaborated for the rest of the year, and I began my classroom library through gifts from other teachers. It was time well spent. I was also asked to join a few teachers on a trip to the school's supply closet (I never would have found it on my own) and to an office supply store that afternoon, which really helped.

Walking the grounds of the school is a good way to get to know important people and to get an overview of the physical school, too. See if the office has a map of the building. If not, sketch the school on your clipboard as you walk and write down who teaches where. Mark the area of the upper- and lower-grade classes. Note the locations of the school psychologist, the social worker, the guidance counselor, the specialist teachers, and art, music, and dance teachers. All will be places where you will bring or send students. Here's the essential: Star all the restrooms in case you are visiting another class with your students and someone needs to go. And remember, that includes you as well. Know where the teacher restrooms are.

The Art of the Stolen Idea

As you walk the grounds and get to know other teachers, gather any advice and ideas from those teachers that you can. Do they have any tricks or routines they use to start the year on a positive note? Do they have strategies they use during read-aloud time to increase comprehension?

Do they have a great way to teach math or to get kids to walk down the hall quietly? Maybe they have a tried-and-true homework system that is different from yours. This is one of the best ways to improve your own practice. Start "pilfering" ideas before the first day of school.

I steal ideas throughout the year, not just at the beginning. My teaching style is a patchwork of ideas and concepts I've learned from other teachers. Take a prep period and watch a friend teach or just stop by and look around someone's classroom. Bring your lunch to the classroom of a colleague who teaches a different grade and/or subject and see what you can learn. Great teaching is all about continuing to learn. Make it a yearlong—and lifelong—experience.

DAY-TO-DAY ROUTINES AND RULES

A large part of a school's culture has to do with its everyday routines and rules, like how to handle absences and what you're expected to do with students when school lets out. These are the nitty-gritty details—often mundane and sometimes a pain—that, when added together, make up the rhythm of daily life in your school. If you learn them early on, you'll have fewer surprises and less stress in the first few weeks.

Absence and Lateness

You'll most likely get an attendance sheet to turn in or access to an online attendance system to mark kids late or absent. Find out what your school's system is and how to use it, but also find out:

- Your responsibility with regard to extended absences. Should you email the families after a certain number of absent days, or will the school do that for you? (If I think there is a problem with a child's attendance, I call the home to find out what is going on. If I think there's a family issue that's keeping the child home, I tell the guidance counselor and social worker—in a hurry.)

- What to do if you've turned in your sheet and a kid you marked as absent walks through the door. The school may want you to send him back to the office to get a Late Pass or you may be required to submit a Late Pass yourself later on in the day. Find out.

I had a student who transferred into my class from another school a month into the year. When I read her records, I noticed she had been absent more than 50 days the year before. I called her previous school to get the background before discussing it with the family, but the people I spoke with had no idea why she had missed so many days. I asked her mother about the absences, and she said her daughter, who was in third grade at the time, had been mistakenly going to a fifth-grade class. The fifth-grade teacher figured she was an extra student, or didn't notice, and her third-grade teacher continued to mark her absent. The mother was working three jobs, and the grandmother, who spoke no English and was doing all of the homework with the child, was concerned that the work was so hard. Of course it was! She had skipped two grades! Moral of the story: It's always worth it to investigate if a student shows an exorbitant number of absences. And—though it may seem obvious—always keep track of who is in your class and who shouldn't be.

BTW: Many teachers are tough on a student for being late, but it's not always the student's fault. Before you come down on a kid for being late, find out what the reason is. Most kids are eager to get to school and can usually move mountains (their families) to get there. In elementary school, the vast majority of the time it's the family's fault when a student is late. If you have a student who is late a lot, talk to the parents and help them understand the importance of getting their child to school on time. Maybe you could share some ideas with them or find some resources to help them get their child to school on time. Be encouraging to the student when he or she shows up on time.

Sickness and Substitutes

Just like your students, you are likely to get sick, too, so make sure you have a substantive, well-written lesson plan ready for a substitute teacher. Include activities that can be easily administered, but make sure the plan has solid content so the kids are learning while you're out.

You need to know:

- The number of sick and personal leave days you're allotted
- The procedure for getting a substitute teacher when you're sick or need to take a personal day
- Whether there is a sub list with contact information for substitute teachers your school regularly employs
- The amount of advance notice your principal requires

BTW: Sometimes a substitute teacher will feel like he or she barely survived the day with your (normally well-behaved!) students, and at the end of the day will push your class right out the door so that he or she can escape as quickly as possible. To prevent any mistakes, be sure you provide a clearly formatted dismissal chart (the class roster you used on the first day of school, see pages 44–46) so the substitute knows who goes where.

If you have a choice, ask around before you choose a substitute teacher for your class. Find out who teachers, kids, and parents like and don't like (and why) and who is good with upper or lower grades. Find out who is known to be kind, aloof, or tough. Then pick the right substitute for your class. If all goes well while you're out, write down the substitute's name so you can contact him or her again. If the school has a substitute list, add the name and book the person in advance for as many days as needed. Nothing makes coming back to school easier than having hired a good sub.

Walking the Halls

Practice walking around the school with your class. This will prove to be valuable when you take a field trip. In addition to teaching kids the rules for how to walk together, you can also use this as a time to tour the building. If you have students new to the school, or if you're teaching students who changed buildings from one grade to another, they might not be familiar with where the restroom is, much less where other classrooms or the offices are.

Restroom Policies

You'll need to know the school rules about students using the restrooms. For instance, can one student go at a time or is a partner required? Do they need a hall pass? Which grades use which restrooms? Where are the restrooms for adults, and are they locked?

And when do *you* go to the restroom? If you have to teach from 8:30 to 12:30 with no breaks, can you just leave your class of kids for a few minutes? Nope! To avoid wrangling with this issue, many teachers put themselves in a perpetual state of dehydration. Here's an easier solution: talk to the teacher across the hall about watching your class while you run down the hallway, or find a teacher who has a break when you don't and have that person sit in for a few minutes. Otherwise, well, um, you might be in for some trouble and will be using those spare clothes you left in the closet a lot sooner and more often than you thought!

Lunchtime

Find out what your responsibilities are so you get your class to the right place at the right time. You need to know:

- Whether you need to walk all the kids down to the cafeteria and wait until everyone is seated
- Whether "hot lunch" kids go to one place and "bag lunch" kids go to another area
- Whether kids are allowed to eat in your room with you
- What the procedures are for kids who receive lunch through a government program
- What happens on half days
- If you are responsible for finding out about food allergies and telling the cafeteria staff

On my first day in a new school, I brought my students down to the cafeteria for lunch in a quiet line—a true victory. I waited for a moment and left them there with a lunch aide, as I had done the year before in the other school where I had taught. Seeing what I had done, my principal walked over to me. "Mr. K," she said in a soft voice, "my expectation of you is that you bring your class down and make sure everyone is at least on their way to getting their lunch before you leave. I don't have the staff here to monitor that many children and the extra moment you spend here will make a big difference." Point made. I followed her direction each and every day after that. Find out what the expectation is in your school.

BTW: It always pays to walk your class to the cafeteria or recess, whichever they go to first, and spend time with them. The extra moments I spend at the beginning of the year, helping either in the lunchroom or in the school yard, are recognized both by my students and by the recess and cafeteria staff who are always overworked and appreciative of the needed help. If you make this effort, then when you're late to pick up your class, you can be pretty sure they'll have your back. And don't forget to eat your own lunch! You not only deserve a break, but also need fuel for the rest of the day.

Inclement Weather Procedure

Find out what happens in case of stormy weather. Are you required to conduct recess in your classroom? Are morning drop-off and afternoon dismissal held in different locations from usual?

Whatever the procedure, always have a number of games and other activities in your classroom in case your kids spend recess indoors with you. These are also very useful during a time when you give kids the choice to play games or do different activities in your class. And yes, those math manipulatives count as fun things to play with, too!

Communication

Before the beginning of the year, I give my cell phone number to three people: my principal, the school secretary/office manager, and a grade-level colleague. As the year progresses, I also give it to friends I've made. I never give my personal number to students' parents. Similarly, I always have a work email, like most people, but I keep my personal email separate and private. I recommend you do the same, but also find out if your school requires you to give your number to anyone.

Talk to your mentor or a colleague to find out how staff at your school communicates, too. Can you text your principal if you're running late? Are announcements and other communications sent out mainly by email, or will you get slips of paper in your office in-box? You'll want to find out how your principal feels about teachers on social media, too. A good rule of thumb is to have tight personal boundaries. Think twice about being a "friend" of a student on social media (I wouldn't), and if you blog about your personal experiences in the classroom, know that many people in your school community may read it. I advise against it.

Let Them Know Before You Go

You're going to be a part of a very large community that includes your fellow teachers, your principal and other staff, your students, and their families. If you take your class somewhere, even if only to the school library, com-puter room, or playground, all these people need to know where you have gone. Make some sort of sign or system to inform people of your class's where-abouts at all times. Find out what the school uses to keep track of the where-abouts of teachers if they're off campus.

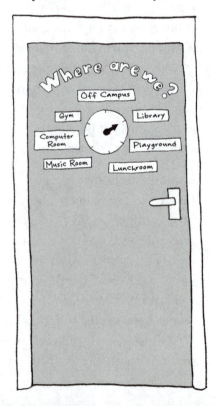

It's also a good idea to write or print out a schedule of when your class goes to music, art, science, gym, or any other special classes. Post it on your door so the school community knows where to find you and your class. You can also add a destination wheel with an arrow that points to where you are, like recess, field trip, gym, or lunch. Get this system ready to go before the first day of school.

It was 1:45 in the afternoon on a terribly hot day in June. The kids were restless so I took them out on the playground to run around in the sun. I had forgotten that a parent was going to pick up her child early to get to a dentist appointment at 3 p.m. When she found an empty classroom and no note on the door, the mother understandably panicked and ran to the office, asking where her son's class was. There was nothing on the calendar. One of the office staff knew I might be in the school yard, but by then the principal and assistant principal were involved. If I had only left a note on the door the situation would have been that much easier for everyone involved—including me.

Technology and Internet

Find out what technology your school has or doesn't have. Are there interactive whiteboards? Are there laptops or tablet devices that you can use to teach? What are you required to know how to use? Is your school a BYOD (Bring Your Own Device) community, where you can use your own technology to teach? Find out, and get familiar with whatever technology is available to you.

Many schools have wireless connections today, and hopefully all will have them soon. Find out what your school or district policy is in terms of Internet searches, use of email, and how you're either required or able to use the Internet in your day-to-day teaching. Can you have a class website? How about a class blog or Twitter account? Can you use YouTube videos in class or apps that connect to the Internet? What about apps that use your location via Google Earth? Technology and Internet access provide many wonderful benefits to teachers and classes, but there are many potential pitfalls to monitor, too. Know your school rules, and be aware of what your kids are doing.

Morning Drop-Off

You need to know where your students are dropped off in the morning and whether they'll find their own way to your door or if you need to pick them up somewhere. You'll also need to know whether things will go differently on the first day of school. For instance, maybe you need to make a sign and meet your class in the auditorium or gymnasium. Maybe parents will walk their kids to your classroom.

> A friend of mine who taught second grade changed schools. On the first day at the previous school, parents would drop off their children at the door of the classroom, maybe spend a few moments saying good-bye, and then leave. In the new school, the parents followed the kids into her classroom and didn't leave. After about 20 minutes, with her class into their first routine, my friend mentioned to the parents that they were free to leave. "But we usually stay for most of the first day," one of the parents informed her. The room was packed. Being savvy, my friend quickly gave the parents things to do, and by 10 a.m. some parents had settled into useful roles while others decided to leave.

Make a class roster in Excel or another program before the first day of school. List the names of your students down the left side of the page and put columns of boxes to the right. Then make a gazillion copies of it and use it as your tracker for everything. On the first few days of school, I bring the roster on a clipboard when I pick up my class at morning drop-off to help me track the students. I also use it as an unofficial attendance chart. I use this roster all year long for other things, like tracking who has brought in a permission slip and paid the attendance fee for an upcoming field trip or who has finished a particular assignment. Sometimes I'll use three or four different columns on the sheet to track student progress on an assignment (one column for outline, one for draft, one for edited draft, and one for final). Bring the roster on the first day and keep it for every class-list record you need.

See page 46 for an example.

After-School Routines

At the end of a hectic day, or even a calm one, dismissal can be confusing. You need to know:

- Where you take the students, including those who take the bus, those who get picked up by a parent, those who walk home alone, and those who go to after-school programs

- Which busses your bussing students are supposed to take; young kids easily forget, especially during the first week

- What measures are in place to make sure kids go with the adult they're supposed to go with

- Where to bring students if their parents are late and who is responsible for waiting with them

- If no one has picked up a child, whether you will need to call a parent or family member

- What happens on half days (and that includes what to do about lunch for your students)

If your school has multiple after-school programs, make a chart for the class indicating who goes where on what day. If a student tells you he's going somewhere other than his usual destination (like someone who normally takes the bus tells you

BTW: Develop a routine so each child checks in with you before leaving for the day. For example, I have every child shake my hand and tell me where they are going (I'll know beforehand but I want them to tell me to confirm they know as well). If it's an adult picking them up, I want to see that person with my own eyes before I let the student leave.

Sample Class Roster

Roster

Purpose: Morning drop-off

Name	12/9	12/10	12/11	12/12	12/13	12/16	12/17
Sam B.	X	X					
Sean B.	X	X					
Jack C.	X	X					
Nick C.	X	X					
Georgia D.		X					
Tiana D.	X	X					
Filah F.	X	X					
James F.	X	X					
Lisa G.	X						
Rose G.	X	X					
Jeremy H.	X	X					
Jasp K.	X	X					
Elaine L.	X						
Gabe M.	X						
Tea M.	X	X					
Linda M.	X	X					
Peta M.	X	X					
Ryan O.		X					
Paul P.	X	X					
Alexis R.	X	X					
Katie S.	X	X					
Miyu S.	X	X					
Rey S.	X						
Kayla V.	X	X					
Diamond W.	X	X					
Jamie W.	X	X					
Jay Z.	X	X					

he's going home with a friend), be sure you have a note from the student's parent before allowing this.

> One year I started at a different school with a lot of after-school programs. All those programs were great for the kids, but being new to the school, I didn't know where each program gathered and who went to which program on what day. The third week of school I made a mistake. A new student told me he had signed up to play games after school. There was a general after-school program, so I brought him there. When the after-school teacher looked on the roster and didn't find the child's name, I explained the student was new to the school, and we both assumed he would be added to the list in the next day or so. About 30 minutes later, the school secretary called me in my classroom to ask where the student was. His after-school program, called "Games," had been waiting for him this entire time and the teacher was not happy. I sheepishly hung up the phone, got the kid from the one program, and brought him to the other. After that, I made a chart of after-school programs.

Field Trips

Field trips are always tricky. Prior to planning your first excursion, you need to know:

- Where to post your trip so the school community knows where you're going and when; most field trips need to be approved by the principal
- If you need to fill out a rationale form tying your trip to your curriculum
- If the district or school has funding for your trip
- Whether or how you can use public transportation with your class
- How to reserve a bus

- If the school has a relationship with any museums, parks, and/or nearby stores
- Whether there are any places where the school established a bad reputation (for example, a class went there and was poorly behaved or something went wrong that was out of the teacher's control)
- Whether there are places you should avoid, such as places with impatient docents or poorly run facilities
- Whether parents are allowed to volunteer and, if so, what the school guidelines are
- Where you get permission slips, who needs to approve them, whether you keep or file copies of them somewhere, and what information needs to be filled in on the district-wide field trip permission slip forms; find out if there are different forms for local field trips where you walk as opposed to trips you take on a school bus or using public transportation
- Whether anyone needs to retain a copy of the field trip forms while you're on the trip
- What adult-to-student ratio is needed for the field trip
- Whether you need to bring basic first aid, and whether you are allowed to administer first aid if a child gets hurt

Before you copy and send home permission slips to be signed, fill in as much of the information on the original as possible (such as location of field trip, date, and departure and arrival time). The less parents have to fill in, the more likely you are to get them back quickly.

BTW: Find out which parents work in restaurants, shops, or businesses that could serve as interesting and relevant field trips for your class.

I always include a local field trip permission slip in the First Day of School Note Home (see page 156). Check to see if your school allows these and, if so, whether it has a version already created. Then, if you want to walk to the park, go outside to study a certain tree near the school, or even run around the block with your class, you don't need to get a permission slip each time. It's already signed and done for the entire year. However, the local field trip permission slip probably can't be used for public transportation, no matter how short the trip.

The most important rule of all is to count your kids before you go, during the visit, and before you leave the venue. Make sure you have all your kids!

Copies

Find out if you need to drop off originals to be copied, and if so, where you drop them and how much lead time is needed. You can ask a colleague or the office manager. Also find out who is in charge of the copier and of making copies, and be sure to treat this person nicely. You might even present this person with a gift once a year, like a little box of chocolate with your stack of copies, to show your appreciation. Just make sure the person can see it. A melted chocolate truffle on the copier will make you enemy number one, especially since getting a copy machine repair person to school can be as hard as changing the weather.

If you're expected to do your own copying, you'll need to find out the procedure for that. Are you supposed to bring your own paper, or does the school supply it?

Schools usually have several copiers. Find them. Look around and ask people where they are, but be sure to find one copier that you can use in a jam. It beats running to the local copy shop. That said, try not to rely upon copies for your entire

BTW: Always keep five or six reams of paper in your classroom, even if your school supplies paper for copying. Someday the office or another colleague will run out, and you will be the Good Samaritan by saving the day.

lesson. You'll find that many days the copier will be out of order or in the middle of a big job that you can't interrupt, leaving you in a bind. Often you'll have online forms to print, so you'll also want to find out what printers you can use for that.

Although I also have seen many teachers buy small copiers for their room, I wouldn't recommend that. You'll be spending a lot of money on toner and other supplies out of your own pocket and, not surprisingly, a lot of other teachers will want to use it, too. The noise of copies being made in the back of your room by your best friend who teaches across the hall is distracting and your copier will break as often as the school's.

Bulletin Boards

Every school has varying requirements for bulletin boards. Some school districts require certain permanent items, such as phonics guidelines, math operations, and standards, to be displayed on either bulletin boards or classroom walls. Some principals are happy to let the teachers decide for themselves what to display. Others want them changed every month, some every two weeks, and a few, it seems, want them reworked every week and to resemble an exhibit at the Louvre.

BTW: Try covering your bulletin boards with fabric instead of paper. It won't tear so you won't need to replace it for every new assignment. It'll save you a lot of time.

In addition to these big-picture requirements and expectations, find out your school's guidelines for work presented on a hallway bulletin board. Usually, work posted on bulletin boards in the hallway is expected to have gone through a few drafts or edits. This work may also need to be clearly labeled with the subject area and topic (for example "Math, Fractions"). In some cases, a bulletin board is designated for each subject.

TEACHING AND STUDENT ASSESSMENT

You'll want to wrap your mind around the academic part of the job as soon as possible. That means if you're required to use a certain curriculum, get as familiar with it as you can. Find out if it's dictated by the state, district, or your school, and find out how much freedom you have to work creatively within it. As you develop your skills as a teacher, you'll be able to personalize curriculum more and more. It's also helpful to find someone you can collaborate with to help you get on the right track in terms of using and modifying the curriculum.

One of the most important things to do both at the beginning of the year and throughout the year is to assess your students. It's your opportunity to find out what they know in different subject areas. This is essential because it helps you understand what they need to review, how to differentiate the curriculum for certain students, as well as how to group them appropriately. It's an ongoing process, knowing where they are in terms of their understanding of various curriculum and material. The two kinds of assessments to be aware of are *summative* assessments—which include state and district assessments, end-of-unit or chapter tests, and end-of-term or semester exams—and *formative* assessments—which include conversations you have with the student, observations you make, or other informal assessments you make in the midst of a curriculum or unit.

The assessments you use to help you understand your kids are different from assessments the district or school may use to show progress. Find out which assessments are used by your grade-level colleagues for each. Are they created by the district or within your school? Does each grade level make its own, or are they more formalized? When do you administer them, and for which subjects? Are they assessments that must be administered one-on-one, like taking running records while reading, or are they administered to the entire class? And how many times per year?

Summative assessments, particularly those administered by the state, can also be used to assess a teacher's effectiveness. These standardized tests are usually taken later in the year and the scores are not released for at least a few weeks. In some schools, a lot of pressure can be placed on teachers to prepare students for the state tests. Some teachers do test preparation all year, while some do none. Take the temperature in your school to see how tests are dealt with.

Teacher Assessment

You'll be assessed, too, so be ready for that. Part of that will most likely involve data from student assessments, and another part involves being observed by your principal or representatives from the district. You can read much more about how to have an awesome observation on page 210, but before school begins, you'll want to find out:

- If you'll be observed and, if so, when and by whom
- How test scores, portfolios, student work, and other factors affect your assessment
- What you can do to help prepare the observer, such as showing him or her lesson plans, curriculum plans, or notes about individual students

Report Cards

The procedure teachers follow to complete reports cards can vary among districts and even among schools within a certain district. In some schools, you have the freedom to add sections, while in others the format is fixed. In some districts, report cards are completed entirely online. Distribution of report cards differs from school to school as well, with some schools requiring that you send them home with kids, some schools having you mail them, and others using an online delivery system.

You need to know:

- When the reporting periods are
- If report cards are based upon a narrative, letter or number grades, or a mix; if necessary, use last year's model so you have an idea what to expect
- If your school uses a computerized program, and if so, who can teach you how to use it
- Whether you're required to submit report cards to your principal or assistant principal before you send them to families
- Whether to share with students their grades before report cards go home
- If there's someone who is willing to review reports containing sensitive or difficult news

One year I handed out all my report cards along with a brief note asking families to sign and return them to me. But I only received about half of them back and had to rewrite the others, which, you can imagine, was not a great use of my time. I never did that again. From then on, I made photocopies of the report cards and sent those home. I had parents sign the original at the parent-teacher conference, which I kept until the end of the year. The signed or unsigned card was also a record of whether the parent attended the conference.

BTW: At the beginning of the year, ask each family to provide you with three or four self-addressed stamped envelopes so you can pop report cards in the mail instead of sending them home with students. That way you are pretty much guaranteed they'll make it home.

GETTING TO KNOW THE PARENTS

Talk to teachers who have been at the school for a while about the parent population. Are parents heavily involved at your school? Can you expect them to stop by your room occasionally, or will you rarely see them? Are parents allowed to enter the school at any time of day to visit, or do they need to request a pass? If so, is the pass approved by you? Does your school encourage parents to drop off kids at the front of the school or allow them to come in with their children? Is there a certain time in the morning when all parents should be gone?

First Day of School Note Home

Many schools have materials that you are required to send home on the first day or two of school. These include many forms that students' families need to fill out and send back, including emergency contact information, lunch forms, after-school registration, and more. Find out what those forms are so you can make your packet early and then add the following, also to be filled in by the family and returned:

- Basic information sheet with names of all family members with whom the child lives
- Local field trip permission slip (see pages 48–49)
- Space where parents can share information they think is important about their child
- Parent volunteer sheet—this will help you understand who is available and when, as well as what parents can do to help

See page 169 for an example of a First Day of School Note Home.

Back to School Night or Meet the Teacher Night

Some schools have an agenda they want you to follow, and other schools will let you conduct your meeting as you please. Some schools get great turnout, others not so much. Don't wait to learn about Back to School

Night—ask around to find out. You'll need to know when it occurs, how long the meeting should last, whether you need to hand out any paperwork, and what topics you're expected to cover. Talk to some of the other teachers in your grade level, plan with them, and find out what the meetings are typically like in terms of attendance and tone. You can read a lot more about Meet the Teacher Night on page 179.

Parent-Teacher Conferences

Schools vary on how to manage parent-teacher conferences. You need to know when they take place, how long they should be, and whatever paperwork you're required to have for the meeting, such as report cards and/or student work. Find out if interpreters are available at school in case you need one.

You can read a lot more about how to prepare for parent-teacher conferences on page 191.

PTA/PTO

The Parent-Teacher Association or Organization can be a powerful governing body at many schools, and the decisions it makes can affect the culture of the school in sometimes significant ways. It also raises money for the school. You need to know:

- Who is on your PTA or PTO, what they do, and what they've done in the past
- Whether you should attend any meetings that relate directly to school practices

RESPONSIBILITIES BEYOND THE CLASSROOM

Teachers have many responsibilities beyond day-to-day teaching, from professional development for yourself to managing extracurricular activities and celebrations. Your principal, secretary, and fellow teachers can provide information about these—find out what's expected of you early on.

Committees

Most schools have a committee that keeps track of social items such as who's getting married, expecting a baby, retiring, moving, celebrating a birthday, or other events, including illnesses, deaths, and even tragedies. This committee keeps everyone in the loop about these events and, when appropriate, arranges small parties or gives a gift. Other committees might be responsible for school safety or leadership. Think carefully about your interests and what type of time commitment you want to make, especially in your first years of teaching. A committee that works with issues of school leadership is probably going to be more of a workload than the committee in charge of special events for teachers. You may be eager to learn the ins and outs of the school, but it's a good rule of thumb not to sign up for more than one committee at first or you may find yourself spending way too much time at meetings and not focusing enough on your students.

Often you don't have a choice about the committees you serve on. They may be appointed or be a rite of passage for new teachers. Some you'll want to be a part of if you want to become more involved in school leadership in the future.

You need to know:

- If you're required to participate on a committee
- What committees there are and how to choose the one(s) you want
- How many times the committee meets and what your responsibilities are
- Who is on what committee (if possible, you don't want to join a committee with a person you find hard to work with)

Meetings, Conferences, and Professional Development

You're going to have a lot of different meetings to attend as well as the opportunity to attend conferences and professional development workshops (some required). To navigate these responsibilities successfully, you'll need to know:

- When meetings—including staff, grade-level, and union—take place and where. You might be required to host a meeting in your classroom. If so, be sure to clean up your room before the meeting. It's not pleasant to meet in a classroom that smells like rotten food, where the floor is sticky from an art project or you can't put your elbows on the table because it's covered with paint and unidentifiable liquids.

- If you're required to attend any staff development workshops and when they're held. They usually take up a half day or full day during the week, but sometimes they're held on Saturdays, before or after school, or over multiple days. Find out and mark them on your calendar so you don't schedule a field trip or other class event on those days.

- Whether professional development is required and whether the school pays for it. Professional development can be very valuable regardless. It's a great way to improve your knowledge and skills as a teacher, meet and learn from teachers from other schools, and advance your career.

Fundraisers

Different schools have different rules and expectations about when, where, and how classes can raise funds. Find out if you're allowed to do bake sales and if there are any restrictions around that. Do you need to sell prepared foods? Is it preferred that you sell arts and crafts or a class newspaper?

If it's allowed, be creative with how you fundraise. Bake sales work okay if they're allowed (in some districts they're not), but the school community will appreciate it if you do something new that benefits everyone. If you work with a population that cannot afford to support a fundraiser, approach businesses in the community. Explain what it's for, and you might find people who are happy to contribute.

> I held bake sales my first few years of teaching but didn't like the fact that I was pumping students full of sugar, so one year I changed tactics and asked parents to cook and help sell chili for a community fundraiser. The ingredients are inexpensive, so even if a parent couldn't afford to make an entire pot she could donate some cheese, sour cream, beans, or hot sauce, and different families could provide different flavors and styles: spicy, not-so-spicy, meaty, veggie, beans, no beans, and so on. It was a huge hit, and we made a lot of money to support our end-of-the-year field trip. I also used it as a chance to talk about what makes a healthy diet, as well as studying where the food came from.

Graduation

Some schools hold a graduation ceremony for kindergarten students, some hold one for kids graduating to middle school, and some hold ceremonies for kids finishing every grade. If your students will be participating in a graduation ceremony, find out where and when it's held and what kind of turnout you can expect. Is it a big deal in this community? What are your responsibilities? If your grade level doesn't have a graduation ceremony, what are you expected to do to mark the end of the year, if anything?

Holidays and Birthdays

Find out what holidays are celebrated at your school, including which ones the school closes for and which ones you observe at school. Private and public schools may vary in terms of days when school is closed. It's important to know before the school year begins. Talk to colleagues to find out if you might have students, such as Jehovah's Witnesses, who do not celebrate a holiday that the school honors in daytime celebrations. If that's the case, how have other teachers handled that? The school may have a policy.

On a similar note, decide how you want to acknowledge birthdays in class. I like to offer parents the opportunity to send in a treat that the child can pass out at the end of the day. Check what your school allows first;

BTW: If you teach the final grade at a school (for example, fifth grade in a K–5 school), you may be giving families portfolios of their child's work from all of their years at the school at the end of the year. Before you do this, go through it to make sure no notes are written by previous teachers that the parents shouldn't see, like comments to the next year's teacher about how difficult the child is or how the parents were not cooperative. You want to consider the student and family and protect your fellow colleagues and the school.

the school may have a policy regarding sugary snacks, nuts, homemade foods, or other issues. Be aware of any students who have food allergies or diabetes.

School Performances, Trips, and Functions

Find out before the year starts if you have holiday celebrations or performances to prepare for, a school-wide field day, an auction or fundraiser your class is required to make something for, or various other functions. Mark these events in your lesson book and on a calendar so you're prepared.

> It was my first year of teaching, and I was feeling great about the beginning months even though I was struggling to keep my head above water, just like other new teachers. I was looking forward to a few days off for Thanksgiving when a colleague asked me what I was doing for the Thanksgiving performance. "The what?" I replied, blindsided. I had three days to find some sort of song and dance for my class to do. It was super stressful. We got it done, but instead of peacefully gliding into the long holiday weekend, I was exhausted. If I'd known about it earlier, I would have been prepared—and would have felt much more relaxed that week.

Calendar of Events

Your school likely has a central calendar where all field trips, meetings, and other special events are posted. Find out where it is, how events are added to it, and whether you're required to add anything to it. The office manager typically maintains the school calendar. It may sound obvious, but don't add, delete, or change anything on the school calendar if someone else is in charge of it.

> **BTW:** Consider hosting a classroom-specific calendar of events on the school or class website that lists things such as class field trips, conferences, and meetings. This is a great way to easily share information with parents, school administrators, and colleagues.

Emergencies and Drills

Every school has a protocol for emergencies such as a severe injury to a child, a potentially dangerous person entering the building, a problem with the building, or a disaster in the local area. Be proactive in learning what your school's protocols are. Will an announcement be made over the P.A. system? Are codes used for certain emergencies so students won't be scared?

Determine what staircase, exit, and/or doorway you should take and where your class is supposed to line up during a fire drill. Your whole school will practice emergency drills, but I like to walk the route with my class before the first emergency drill, so the kids know where they're going and how they're expected to behave. If you don't rehearse it'll be like herding grasshoppers.

A SCHOOL WHERE YOU FIT—AND THAT FITS YOU

Once you've met the Big Four, other staff, and most of your fellow teachers, and once you've found a mentor and learned as much as you can about the rhythm and rules of your school, you'll start to become a known entity in the building instead of a stranger. In addition to being exciting and fun, the first days of school can be stressful. But if you're prepared, you won't sweat it too much. Because of the work you've already put in, you'll be ready.

Chapter

THREE

Setting Up for a Terrific Year

If you wander through a school before opening day, you'll find an exhibition of the different rituals that teachers perform before the flood of children pour into their classrooms. Some decorate their rooms, while others rearrange furniture over and over again. Several appear to do nothing but casually sip coffee, read the paper, and talk about their summer, while more than a few chat on their phones and stress out. Some sharpen crayons. (I know. It's a strange habit. Maybe it helps them relax.)

Once your room is set up, you can reduce the stress of the looming first day by turning your attention to some of the classroom practices that'll help you down the road. This chapter outlines simple systems and ideas that will save time, energy, and sanity as you make your way through the roller-coaster ride of the school year. Most importantly, they'll help you and your students be more successful. Once the school year starts, you may be overwhelmed with the number of tasks you'll be assigned and goals you'd like to accomplish, so having systems in place, such as how to manage homework, lost pencils, and scrap paper, will save you hassle, worry, and time, leaving you more free to accomplish what you came to this profession for: to teach kids.

These are the systems and tricks I use, but you'll want to adjust them to work for you. After all, it's your classroom!

THE DAILY SCHEDULE

In all my years teaching, I have never started a day without the daily schedule written on the board. Actually, I never leave my classroom at the end of the day without writing the schedule for the next day. The schedule reminds me of what I intend to accomplish. It's a helpful habit for several reasons.

I always write the complete date at the top and add the abbreviated version (for example 11/16/13) so kids begin to recognize that as a common way to communicate the date. Below that I write the schedule with the time in a left-hand column and the activities in a corresponding right-hand column. Your students will quickly get in the habit of reading the schedule when they enter the room each morning to see what they'll be doing. Immediately they're involved in the plan for the day, and they can ask questions or share excitement or misery (hopefully not) with their classmates.

You can handwrite the schedule on a dry-erase board or display it on your interactive whiteboard, but you'll want it in a place where it is visible all day.

One teacher I knew made the daily writing of the date into a math problem. She always put the current day of school over the total number of school days (for example 23/180). Students would have to figure out how many days were left in the school year. Later on in the year, when it was 90/180, she would use this technique to teach fractions (90/180 = ½). "So, if the year were a pizza, we'd have eaten this much," she would point out. The kids loved it and the countdown got to be pretty exciting when the number of days remaining got into the teens and lower.

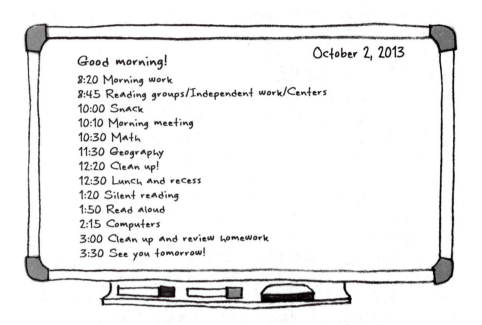

Good morning!   October 2, 2013

8:20 Morning work
8:45 Reading groups/Independent work/Centers
10:00 Snack
10:10 Morning meeting
10:30 Math
11:30 Geography
12:20 Clean up!
12:30 Lunch and recess
1:20 Silent reading
1:50 Read aloud
2:15 Computers
3:00 Clean up and review homework
3:30 See you tomorrow!

The posted schedule is meant to be flexible. Just as you might change plans with a friend, you learn to make adjustments. If one lesson runs over time, cross out another lesson you don't think you'll get to that day, or stop your current lesson and finish it later. If you want to do something later in the day than originally planned, circle it and make an arrow to the new time of day when it's to be done. Don't let the schedule rule you. Use it to keep you and your students on top of a busy day. And if you overplan, which is better than under-planning, you'll have activities that can be carried over into the next day or even later in the week.

BTW: Once you get in the habit of posting the daily schedule the day before, some of your students may begin to ask you if they can help. It's a great end-of-the-day job for kids.

THE LESSON PLAN

Your principal may ask you to defend your lesson plan, which can feel frightening and challenging. But this will help you more clearly understand why you're teaching certain concepts when you're teaching them. As I planned more and more, I learned to think sequentially—for example, I came to know that teaching a certain concept in October would enable me to teach a follow-up or extension in December. I was tracking how I would help students build up to a new skill. This is called scaffolding—providing sequential support to facilitate a student's development.

Your lesson plan book is where you will record all of your lessons in sequential order, but you may also have to write more detailed plans, clearly showing the goal, objective, and method of assessment for each specific lesson. Be sure you understand what you're required to do.

My first year of teaching, my principal asked the new teachers to turn in our lesson plan books for the following week every Thursday by 4:30 p.m. Every Wednesday and Thursday afternoon, I would plan with one of my colleagues. Our plans had to include the following:

- Each lesson

- The objective of the lesson

- The academic standard we were addressing

- The method of assessment used to evaluate learning

- The materials needed

- The time allotted

- Any meetings with parents, field trips, or other special activities and the rationale or reason for each

It would take a few solid hours of work, and we would grumble our way through, fearful of being told we didn't know what we were doing.

> The next afternoon our lesson plan books would be returned, filled with notes and comments about our lessons. It was terrifying at first, but after a while, I began to look forward to it because I realized it was teaching me how to plan. Having someone critique my lesson plan every week taught me what would or wouldn't work and how far in advance to schedule. It also prepared me for being observed or evaluated and made me feel more comfortable defending what I was doing and why.

The thought and effort you put into planning will directly impact your success as a teacher. If you're concerned about planning, find a more experienced teacher to help you when you need it throughout the year. It's worth it. Keep your daily plans, too. They will prove useful as you continue through your career. I co-taught for six years at New York University with a professor named Joe, a brilliant and inspired educator. A veteran elementary school teacher, he would type up each day's plan and post it at the front of the room. And what did he have after years of teaching? An archive of 20-plus years of lesson plans. He could look back and see which ones he might reuse, get ideas from former years, and easily share them with colleagues. Due to the lack of technology, this wasn't the easiest thing to do when he began teaching. Nowadays, it's as easy as peeling a potato.

THE MORNING MEETING

The Morning Meeting has long been viewed as sacred—the most important part of the day. It's the time when the schedule and calendar are reviewed, topics of the day discussed, and important announcements made. It's a crucial time of the day for many reasons, one of the most significant being that it builds community.

Like you, I'm guessing, I was taught that this meeting would get the day off to a good start. But the Morning Meeting was often frustrating for me because of a lack of attendance and late-arrivers. This wasn't a good start for anybody. I would be annoyed, repeating myself, and half the kids arriving late would have no idea what was going on. Start. Stop. Repeat. Start again. Repeat. Stop. I tried using incentives, like an extra snack, fancy pencils, and more free time to get the kids to school on time, but nothing worked.

Finally, after watching a few of my colleagues, I had the courage to challenge what I had been taught. Why hold the Morning Meeting before anything else? It doesn't make sense.

I shifted the Morning Meeting to just after 10 a.m., when I knew everyone who was coming to school that day would be in the room. I got better attendance at the meeting and better attention because nobody was coming in halfway through distracting everyone.

So what did the kids do first thing in the morning? Independent work. They came in, dropped off their homework, hung up their coats, put their lunches away, and got right to work without disturbing anyone else in the class, even if they were late.

Moving the meeting changed the classroom energy in the morning. Instead of dealing with a bunch of squirmy kids struggling to settle down and pay attention, I had a room brimming with productivity. When parents decided to stay for a few moments to watch, they kept their voices low because they could see this was a busy environment and they didn't want to get in the way. Often parents were impressed by how seriously their kids took their work. It also gave me time to speak with specific students and parents as well as complete various duties such as taking attendance, checking in homework, and collecting permission slips or other forms that were due. But most importantly, it taught the kids how to be independent and responsible for themselves. Morning Meeting? Just call it Meeting Time and make it happen later in the day.

MORNING INDEPENDENT WORK

If you follow my suggestion to push back the Morning Meeting and assign independent work first thing in the day, make sure the activities you assign are not too easy or half your class will finish in five minutes and start throwing paper airplanes around the room (or asking you what to do next). If the work is too difficult, it won't get done. Find a balance. You can assign different types of activities, from math problems to spelling words, journal assignments to art projects, or make it a time to finish up previously assigned work. These activities aren't meant to be "time killers," so make sure they directly relate to whatever you're teaching. Have kids practice skills you've previously introduced. And differentiate different Morning Work for different groups of kids, too.

Here are two examples of morning work activities:

Fifth grade

1. Do the multiplication math sheet in the yellow basket.

2. Please answer the following journal question: If you could create a special, superhuman power, what would it be? Why? What would you do with it? Where?

3. Read quietly.

First grade

1. Copy the spelling words from the board.

2. Do the Math Problem of the Day.

3. Write in your journal: What is your favorite color, and why?

4. Go to your center.

After students finish their work, allow them to go to independent learning centers or meet with you for small group instruction.

> **BTW:** Some teachers give a series of problems for the week and the kids work through them as the week progresses. That way everyone stays challenged and no one is bored.

EXTRA WORKSHEETS

I always have a stack of extra worksheet assignments in the classroom, such as maps to fill in, math problems, and spelling review. Why? In your first years of teaching you'll undoubtedly run into gaps in your day when you just didn't plan enough. That 20-minute span before lunch can seem like an eternity if you don't have a quick activity to do. And what if your sub ends with 90 minutes left and decides to give free art time? You'll come in the next day to a classroom that looks like a herd of bulls trampled through it. Tell the sub to use the stack of handouts. Or what if you get pulled out of your class in the middle of the day for an emergency meeting and a sub is sent in on the spur of the moment? Grab some work from the pile and give it to him or her. This is not meant to be busywork, and it won't be if you keep it tied to the curriculum. Keep it fresh by updating the pile regularly.

> I had just finished my mid-morning meeting with my class of first graders when a member of the office staff came into my classroom with nine second graders in tow. "We couldn't get a sub so can you take these kids for the day?" "Of course," I responded, "but do they have work to do?" They all nodded, and proceeded to finish their work in 15 minutes. It was 10 o'clock. Thankfully, I had a stack of extra worksheets, which I promptly gave to them. That material kept them busy and engaged while I finished my class's lesson. At lunch I was able to regroup and figure out a way to include the guest students in our afternoon work.

I also keep a stack of Mad Libs, counting and math games, and even childhood games like hangman. When you have just 10 minutes and you need an activity fast, these will save you.

ORGANIZING STUDENT WORK

So what do you do with all of the work that your students produce? Where do they put it without your room turning into a tornado of paperwork?

For lower grades, I have students keep one folder per subject area in their desks or in boxes throughout the classroom, usually near an area that relates to that specific subject area (like math folders near the math manipulatives). They keep their classwork, projects, and homework that I return to them in those folders. Once every week or 10 days I sit with each child and we go through the folders. I have them choose the pieces of work they are most proud of and I place those in their portfolio (see page 71). They keep in the folder any work for current projects, and take home or throw out anything that we both deem unnecessary to keep, such as a set of addition problems that they know how to do. This procedure keeps what is important in the classroom, teaches the kids how to choose what they feel is their best work for the portfolio, and routinely removes a lot of unnecessary paperwork.

> Early in my teaching career, I was going through a first-grade student's folder, pulling out what I thought was his strongest work. He asked me what I was doing, and I said, "Finding your best work." He looked at me and said, "How do you know if it really is my best work? I did it. I might know better than you." He was right. Since then, I've never looked at students' work the same way. I always involve the students or follow their lead in the discussion. We may have differences of opinion, but I always dedicate myself to listening to their rationale.

For older kids, I use a binder system, which is divided by subject areas such as science, math, reading, writing, spelling, projects, and anything else that seems necessary. They file all of their work in their binder. Again, just as with the younger grades, don't let the binder become a home for clutter. Periodically go through it with the student to decide what stays in there, what is filed in the permanent portfolio, what is sent home, and what is recycled.

STUDENT PORTFOLIOS

Every school is different in terms of what it requires or expects in a student portfolio. Some have a detailed file folder system, where you keep student work samples. Others have no system at all yet will expect you to keep perfect records. There is one thing to remember, no matter what the system: *Keep copies of student work!*

Set up a file for each student. Fill it with relevant notes about work or classroom behavior, as well as *significant* work samples such as classroom projects, artwork, homework, tests, quizzes, and other assessments. Don't just fill it up with every assignment students complete. If you do, the file folders will weigh a ton by the end of the second month of school. Rather, include work that shows their best effort, progress they have made, struggles they continue to have, and assessments.

If you're sending home originals, put a copy in the student's file. And get a small date stamp; it will come in handy during your career as a teacher. Stamp the date on important notes and student work so you can keep track of progress or areas that continue to need improvement.

> **A team of observers from the district was reviewing our school. They went over everything with a fine-tooth comb and made classroom visits to observe teaching methods and strategies—and to check student work for progress. They visited the classroom of a colleague**

who had not been keeping good records. She fumbled through her mostly empty files (it was already February), sweating as she tried to fudge her way through the observation. She was miserable, and our principal was equally unhappy. My colleague ended up being grilled not only by the team of observers, but also by the principal.

That lengthy explanation you prepare to explain how a child is doing will mean nothing if you have no evidence to back up your words. If a principal asks me for a student's work samples from the fall, I can pull them easily. If a parent wants to see proof of her child's progress, I can find examples of that, as well.

HOMEWORK

Homework is a constant battle for teachers, parents, and students alike. You spend hours organizing, making copies, forming little packets, or stuffing folders when you could be doing something else potentially more productive. It may seem like your students, and even some of their parents, think homework is a waste of time and paper, and you'll hear lots of excuses for not doing it ("the dog ate it," "my little sister spilled her juice on it"). So be sure you have well-thought-out reasons for assigning homework and a solid system for assigning, storing, collecting, and correcting it.

Why Give Homework?

Some schools assign a lot of homework and others don't give any. Some teachers give more than others—and even send it to parents. You'll have to find out what the norm is at your school.

I have three reasons why I give homework. They are to help students:

- Memorize facts, like multiplication tables or states
- Review something taught in class on a given day
- Begin or continue work on a project

If the homework I'm considering doesn't align with one of those reasons, then I don't assign it. I don't believe in giving homework that I wouldn't find useful myself. For each assignment, include a sentence to explain why you've assigned the homework (such as "This will help make addition second nature"). If parents and/or students understand the point of the evening work, they won't feel that it's a waste of time and they'll put energy into it. No one wants to put effort into completing a task or an assignment if it seems useless.

Many teachers give a weekly packet on Monday that is due Thursday or Friday. I like to give homework each night so my students get used to bringing their work home, completing it, and bringing it back the following day. Either system teaches responsibility, which is another good reason to assign homework.

> **BTW:** In most schools, reading at least 20 minutes per evening is a mandatory part of homework. Students fill out a daily reading log that may include a student reflection and a parent signature. Check to see what forms are used in your school and district, but be sure to make reading a part of the evening routine. If a child doesn't appear to be reading at home, find out why and be sure to provide reading time during the day.

The Homework Folder

Don't expect homework stuffed into a backpack or lunch box to be treated seriously. It will arrive home crumpled, looking like a paper airplane that crashed. Put homework and notes for parents, such as announcements or permission slips, in a folder with pockets on either side. Label the left pocket "Communication" and the right pocket "Homework" to keep the paperwork organized. Or better yet, have *the students* label the pockets. Every student gets a folder, and that folder goes home with the student every night and comes to school every morning, where it's placed in the

Homework Folder Bin (see page 75). That way, you'll know where to find the permission slips and any other notes from parents.

Before email, the Homework Folder was one of the only direct routes of communication between you and your students' families. Although many schools now send most notices via email, many still use paper, and some families don't have regular access to a computer. The folder is an easy method to stay in touch, it teaches students to be responsible, and because it can be decorated, it can look cool, too.

BTW: If you check the Homework Folder each day, you may discover that many families don't read the school-wide notes or letters you send home. These folders can become heavy with all of the notes your students are carting back and forth. If this is the case, it's time to reach out to the family to be sure they're reading the notices in their child's folder. Tell them, after they have read a notice, to keep it at home as a reminder.

It's a good idea to buy a bunch of extra folders at the beginning of the year. Look at dollar stores where you can get them for about 15 cents each. Keep them on a shelf for kids who come in and say, "My little brother spilled his grape juice on my Homework Folder and my dad couldn't take me to buy a new one so I can't take my homework home tonight because I don't have a backpack and it's raining out and I have soccer practice." Solve that problem in two seconds by handing out a new folder. A ripped Homework Folder doesn't show respect for the work going back and forth, so make sure the folders are in good condition and students feel good about them. Replace them as needed.

The Homework Notebook

Each student needs a small notebook to write down the evening's assignment. Call it the Homework Notebook and have kids keep it in their Homework Folders. At some point during the day, write the homework assignment on the board and have students copy it in their Homework Notebook, always including the date. I check each student's list. If it's correct, I initial it and the child puts it in the Homework Folder.

If your students aren't yet capable of reading or writing, make a list of the evening's homework, copy it, pass it out, and then read it off the board while the kids follow along. They can then put the copied assignment in their Homework Notebook or Folder.

Some teachers prefer to create a homework sheet that is handed out every afternoon or at the beginning of the week because doing so doesn't waste time during the day. This can be emailed or sent home in the Homework Folder. Many teachers post the evening's homework assignment on a class website so parents can be more involved and can be sure their child is doing his or her work. Still others have students use a planner to record their assignments as well as summarize topics covered all day. All these are solid options.

The Homework Folder Bin

You need someplace where your students turn in their Homework Folders. I use a large plastic tub and label it the "Homework Folder Bin." The kids come into the classroom, take out their Homework Folders from their backpacks, and put them in the bin. Have them keep their Homework Notebook in their desk or cubby so they are prepared to write down the next homework assignment later in the day.

A slightly more complex system, which is particularly effective with older students, is to have them separate everything out of the Homework Folder. You might have a red bin for the math homework, a yellow bin for notes and permission slips, and a blue bin for other miscellaneous items. Kids turn in the items but keep their folders. Sometimes I have them hand

BTW: Always make five to eight extra copies of each homework assignment and keep them in the Homework Folder Bin. If a student forgot to do his homework or claims to have left it at home or on the bus or swore it was turned in two days before you even assigned it, have him grab a copy out of the Homework Folder Bin and do it right then and there. Or give him an extra copy in his Homework Folder that evening. Similarly, if a kid has been absent for a few days, you can easily give her the homework she missed by reaching into the Homework Folder Bin. At the end of the week, remove the extra copies of the week's assignments and either recycle them or file them.

in their empty folders in a bin, too, so I can stuff them with the new homework before giving them back.

If the content of the bins changes daily, which it probably will, you may want to write on the board where you want each item to go. It can look like this:

Good morning! Please do the following:

1. Put your math homework in the red basket.

2. Put the permission slip for tomorrow's field trip in the blue basket.

The Homework Record Book

Keep track of all the homework assignments in a computer file or a booklet divided by subject. You'll be able to use it to show students and their parents what assignments they missed and what assignments they turned in. If you use a booklet, keep it in the Homework Folder Bin so you'll know exactly where it is every day. You'll never lose it because it is always in the same place.

Checking In Homework

Most of the time I'll check in and correct the homework myself. Then I make piles to divide the class into those who understand the concept, those who are on the fence, and those who need help. I meet with the kids who need support, check in with the kids who are on the fence, and individually congratulate the kids who demonstrated that they understood the assignment as I make my rounds. Sometimes I have these students work with the students who need help.

> I was busy correcting all of my students' homework one afternoon during my second year of teaching when a veteran teacher visited me. He looked at the pile of homework I was correcting. "Don't correct all of that," he said. "In the morning, have them swap with a partner and correct each other's homework as you go over the answers. Then collect it. It's a great way for them to work together, and it gives you a chance to move around the room and see who needs help. It also lets you focus on teaching rather than correcting." I don't use this technique every day, but I do it a lot, as do many other teachers I know.

At the beginning of the year, you will want to record the homework after it's turned in, but later, you can have students do this. I had a colleague who selects one student each month from each table group to pass out papers, collect and recycle papers from the group, and, most critically, check in homework each morning. She gives each of these monitors a 3" x 5" index card where they put a check for each child's completed homework every morning. She asks the monitors to be sure each homework assignment is complete and has a name, and to separate the work (reading logs and math papers in separate stacks, for example). Then, they bring the homework to her work area with the check-in card on top. By the time 15 minutes have passed, she will have looked over the cards and caught the no-shows. It works like a charm, and it puts the responsibility back on the students, where it belongs.

If you teach kindergarten or first grade, you'll need to explain the routine, and walk your students through it, over and over. Pair up students who can help each other.

Returning Homework

Do I return all completed homework to students? No. I only hand back homework if I think it can be used as a resource to help their learning. If they do a substantial science sheet for homework, I will correct it and return it. But if it's a sheet of multiplication problems they got all right, I will acknowledge it and offer them the choice of keeping it or recycling it. This decision, whether they're in first grade or fifth, empowers students to decide what is, or isn't, important to them. You can learn a lot about a child by observing what work he prizes and where he might need encouragement or help.

I share this system with parents as well and they appreciate not having their kitchen flooded with paper every evening. Give homework back to the students, or send homework home that shows what they're learning or how they're improving. Don't just fill their backpacks with papers. It's a waste of time for everybody.

BTW: When you send completed work home with a student, it serves as a public relations announcement for what's happening in your classroom. Make sure you do it judiciously but routinely so families feel connected. I also regularly raffle off charts that I use in class when they're no longer needed in the classroom. Students love it. They go home and get to reteach to their families the subjects the in-class chart enforced.

THE SCRAP PAPER BIN

Classrooms have some strange gravitational force that attracts paper. You'll end up with a wide array of used, or partly used, paper, including notes you find on the classroom floor, assignments that were started but scratched, debris from Homework Folders, old work you meant to recycle but never got rid of, and more. What can you do with all this extra paper besides recycle it?

I put all of that scrap paper in a tub in the front of the classroom and label it the "Scrap Paper Bin." If kids forget their Homework Notebook, they can grab a piece of scrap paper to write the assignment on. If kids want to draw a picture during free time or write a note, they can grab a piece of scrap paper. They can recycle the piece of scrap paper after they use it.

Most importantly, this teaches students how to reuse before recycling, which is a great lesson on its own. Some of my students even started a scrap paper bin at home.

I remember sitting in a good friend's classroom watching him run his kindergarten class like a wizard. Kids were doing all kinds of different activities, from paintings about a recent field trip to playing with blocks. All of a sudden, a kid vomited all over the floor. The essence of calm, the teacher grabbed a stack of old newspapers and book order catalogs and covered the puke, as he said to the class, "No problem. Keep doing what you're doing." The vomit was covered, out of sight and out of mind, the remaining students got back to their work and he was able to help the sick student and call the custodian. After school, I asked him where he got all of that paper. "I just grab the old book catalogs that I don't use, and old newspapers from the recycling bin in my building to start," he told me. "Who has time to do a full cleanup in the middle of the day? I use the paper for everything, even collages!" I grabbed a stack of old newspapers and book catalogs that day. You never know how that scrap paper will come in handy!

RECYCLING PAPERWORK

Paperwork can pile up quickly, including notes from parents, the principal, and the PTA, and communication from local museums, teacher supply companies, book order catalogs, and more. To keep the pile from resembling a Himalayan peak, sort through it while next to the recycling bin. If you don't think you want or need a piece of paper, drop it in the bin before it makes it to your desk (where it's likely to sit in a pile for weeks). If the paper is a pretty color or useful in some way, keep it and file it with your art supplies to be used later—or put it in the scrap paper bin.

If paperwork does make it to your desk, do one of the following:

- Write down the information in your plan book (and recycle that paper)
- Pin it up on a bulletin board for daily reference
- File it in the appropriate folder in your file cabinet
- Create a document on your computer labeled "Ideas for [fill in subject area]" and type in the important idea—then recycle the paper.

If it doesn't fit in one of these areas, get rid of it. A pile of paper is only going to distract you from your work. I've been very guilty over the years of having piles of paper clogging up my work area. It never helped me. Stay light and get rid of excess paperwork. If you realize that you threw something out that you needed, you can usually find someone else who has a copy of it.

THE FILE CABINET

Have you walked into a classroom and seen a behemoth of a file cabinet in the corner? It's three drawers tall, two drawers wide and is as easy to move as a broken-down truck. I had to move one of those for a fellow colleague. It was awful, and eventually we had to take out the drawers, but those were so overstuffed she was forced to remove—and then reorganize—everything when she arrived at her new classroom. Your classroom isn't the reference section of the local library. Use a file cabinet, but don't lose control of it.

Always keep a file cabinet in your classroom to keep lesson plans and copies of worksheets, outlines, and other pieces of paperwork. Keep them separated in sections by subject matter. If, after a few years, you find that you are not using a certain lesson anymore, get rid of it. Keep your files easy to use and not overflowing so you can navigate them quickly and with ease.

BTW: I keep as many of my lessons as I can on an external hard drive or a flash drive with more than 2 GB of memory, which saves paper and space. (Be sure to back up everything on another external drive or a cloud system.) If I need something, instead of looking through file folder after file folder, I plug in the external drive and use the "search" feature, and up it comes. It makes sharing via email far easier as well.

PENCILS

You're going to lose more pencils than you ever imagined. It's one of the many mysteries of the elementary school classroom. In one year, it'll feel like you've gone through a million pencils.

What can you do?

If you have a community supply of pencils (if the school provides them or if you sent a note home asking for donations to a central collection of supplies), wrap the top of each pencil, right below the eraser, with a piece of duct tape so you—and the students—know it's a classroom pencil. Then give each student *only one* pencil on the first day.

At the end of the day, ask your students to return their pencils to an assigned jar. Count them. If they return them all, give a prize or some sort of class reward (extra snack or class points, for instance). If they don't return all of the pencils, create a minor consequence (a minute less of free time) or simply don't give the reward. If you count 28 pencils for 29 students, you can bet several kids are going to be scrambling to find that last pencil. Keep it up as long as you can, only replacing pencils when they're no longer usable.

BTW: Electric pencil sharpeners can be loud and disruptive. Keep one at your desk, but try to use it only before or after school. Otherwise, every time a kid sharpens a pencil in your room it will sound like someone is using a chainsaw. Electric sharpeners can also overheat and break frequently. Use the old-school manual wall- or shelf-mounted sharpeners and keep a few of the plastic handheld ones in your room. If you're using manual wall- or shelf-mounted pencil sharpeners, mount one for left-handed students as well. Watching a left-handed student use a right-handed pencil sharpener is not pretty. Something is bound to be broken, and the kid will probably end up in tears.

I love this system because it encourages a sense of community and teaches responsibility. However, you can also have students bring their own supply of pencils and manage them on their own. You might want to buy a box of inexpensive pencils to hand out to students who lose theirs.

THE NEW STUDENT

I can't remember a school year when I didn't receive a new student at some point after the first few months. It happens. Families move. Schools close. You need to be prepared for the sudden inclusion of a new person (or people).

Entering a classroom as the "new kid" can be scary and uncomfortable. The new students will not know your systems or understand the routines of your classroom. Most of them will need some time to get used to it, and they may be afraid to make a mistake.

Keep spare journals, pencils, erasers, text books, and whatever else students need to have in their desks or cubbies ready for that new kid who walks in the door. She'll feel like you were expecting her. Keep copies of all of the important notes you sent home at the beginning of the year to help parents new to your classroom prepare their child and understand the different systems that you employ. Even if all of this is on your computer, keep hard copies handy in case a new student is brought to your classroom in the middle of a lesson and a parent is present, waiting for some sort of proof that you know what you're doing.

BTW: Don't wait to make contact with your new student's family. Get in touch with them that day, if possible, whether it's by phone or in person at dismissal. If a student arrived in the morning, try to contact the family during your lunch. The office in your school will usually have met the family, but you're the child's teacher. Reach out to let them know how your classroom works and what they should be prepared for. They'll appreciate it.

When I was teaching third grade, a new student entered my classroom midyear carrying a large teddy bear. I thought it was odd at her age, since my other students did not bring their toys or comfort objects to school. I gave the new student all of the material she would need, found her a desk, and involved her in the group activity. When she tried to stuff the bear, which took up half the surface of her workspace, in her desk, I suggested that I would keep it on my desk. She put her head down and started to cry. The kids around her tried to console her and then they stared at me. "Mr. K, come on, give her back her stuffed animal," one of them said to me. "It's her first day." I realized the kids were right. Later that day, when I spoke to the girl's mother, she said that they had moved over 10 times in two years. The stuffed animal was the only consistency she had. The next day, when the bear arrived with her, we made a little space for it in the corner of the room. By the following week, she wasn't bringing it to school. Be sensitive to each situation. Everyone has different needs.

BTW: It never hurts to email or call the former teacher of a student to learn about the student's classroom performance, behavior, family life, and any other tips you can get. If you don't get much information from the teacher, try someone else who worked with the student and can provide you with information.

To integrate new students as quickly as possible, assign two students, preferably a boy and a girl, to be a welcoming party. They can give the new student his materials, help him get settled at his desk, introduce him to other students, point out any classroom "norms" or rules, and show him where the restrooms are (if you don't do this, many frightened kids in the early elementary grades will pee in their pants, and then you'll have a big problem). At a break, give the new student a tour of the classroom and maybe even the school. Later in the day, be sure to introduce him to the class by doing a fun name game or something silly to make him feel at home.

Be sure to involve new students in any community-building exercises you have done prior to their arrival. For younger grades, I had a classroom contract, with guidelines for the classroom that we all agreed to follow, that everyone signed. Inviting new students to sign it helped them feel like they were more a part of the class right away.

IEPs AND SPECIAL EDUCATION

Some of the students in your class will have an Individualized Education Program (IEP). (It may be called something else in your district.) The IEP describes the services that a student is to receive because she has a physical, intellectual, or emotional challenge or disability. The law mandates that the student receives extra support. Students may need extra help in certain areas from you, and they will often receive some sort of push-in or pullout service from a specialist a few times per week. Teachers are legally required to follow a student's IEP, or you can face repercussions.

A wide range of students qualify for an IEP, from a child who needs extra help with handwriting to someone who has a memory retention issue or dyslexia. You may have a child with an emotional challenge who receives counseling, an autistic child who receives social skills coaching and extra academic support, or a child who has been prescribed medication for a physiological issue. IEPs cover a lot of ground.

Whether you're a general education or special education teacher, read the IEP of every student you're responsible for so you know the services your students are mandated to receive, from whom they receive it, and for how long they have been receiving it. This will not only help your students, but it will also make you a more informed, effective teacher.

If you're new to a school, find the professionals who provide special education services. This might include a special education teacher as well as specialists such as an occupational therapist, a speech teacher, a guidance counselor, and a psychologist. Learn the locations of their offices and resource rooms because those are where your students most likely will be receiving their group or individual lessons. Determine if any of the specialists have already worked with your students, and get any information you can about them and your students' learning needs before the first day of school. Doing so will help prepare you to differentiate lessons to fit your students' style of learning.

Most importantly, if you don't understand an aspect of the IEP, find out who is in charge of the IEPs and ask.

BTW: An IEP mandates that a student receive an extra service in a particular area, but it doesn't mean the child won't be successful in school. For instance, a student might be your strongest math and reading student but struggle with things like standing in line due to a sensory processing issue. You may know many successful adults who had special needs and may have received some sort of services when they were younger. My father, a well-known and respected motivational speaker, received speech therapy for a lisp when he was in second grade. And a close friend of mine, now a well-respected copy editor and author, received services for a reading comprehension disability. You can help your students overcome their trouble areas so they can succeed.

I taught for four years in a collaborative team-teaching classroom with two teachers—one general education and one special education. Up to 40 percent of the students had IEPs. The other teacher and I shared almost all duties (though as a general educator, I would not perform

any specific techniques for which I had not received training), and the students with IEPs were integrated into the classroom. Often, when a new student teacher or guest would come into the room, they would ask who were the students receiving special education services. Instead of answering them, I would ask them to tell me. Rarely could anyone pick many out of the mix. That's because those students were entirely integrated into the daily routines of the classroom, just like every other student. And they felt that way as well.

WORKING WITH SPECIALISTS

Students who receive special assistance will usually be pulled from your class. Often, this pullout service will happen at an inconvenient time for you, usually because you're teaching something important that you don't want the student to miss. You can try to schedule your day around pullout services, but if a number of your students receive these services, it may be impossible to schedule them all at good times. Just like trying to plan a field trip for a sunny day, it doesn't always work.

Regardless, be as flexible as you can with the specialist. Many of the specialist's services are mandated by the IEP, so by law they must happen. Specialists generally work with children from several classes, usually two to three days per week and usually at the same time of day. It can be tough for them to create their schedule, but if you cooperate with them, you can usually find a time that works for everyone involved.

To make things easier for yourself, find the specialists before the first day of school

BTW: If you've scheduled a special presentation, a field trip, or some other preplanned event that you don't want a student to miss because of her pullout schedule, talk to the specialist in advance. He may be able to alter his schedule for that day. Give him the opportunity to be flexible.

and try to get a copy of their schedule (although they might still be pulling out their hair trying to create it). If you cannot get the schedule before school starts, request that they forward it to you as soon as it's ready so you can put it in your lesson plan book.

Many specialists occasionally like to push-in to the classroom. This means they work with their student one-on-one in your classroom while you teach, supporting your efforts and connecting your lesson with the skills they've taught the student. I love this—if the student is comfortable with it. Some students may feel embarrassed, and it can be distracting to other students in the class. Many kids appreciate the break from pullout services, though. Make sure it works for the student and your classroom.

Early on, I felt frustrated that I didn't know what was happening when a specialist took my students. They would leave and return to my classroom, and I didn't know what had gone on. It struck me as odd. I was responsible for these students but had no clue what extra support was being provided or what I could do to help. I finally scheduled time during my breaks to visit each specialist and watch, if only for five or 10 minutes, to get an idea of their strategies. Not only did it help me further understand the diagnosed challenges of my students, I learned several new techniques to use with all students that I continued to use throughout my career. Whether it's done occasionally or routinely, watching the specialist teach can be a learning experience.

YOU DON'T NEED TO BE A GENIUS TO USE AN INTERACTIVE WHITEBOARD

Technology plays an increasingly important role in the life of the teacher. Even if you think pencils and paper are the most important learning tools in your room, you can't ignore the technology that is now available to help your students, many of which you probably use every day in your out-of-school life.

Although the majority of teachers entering the career now are quite fluent in the use of technology, I've seen teachers ignore it, using computer tables to store art projects, overhead projectors as reading lamps, or laptops as checkerboards. But technology—such as laptops, tablet computers, interactive whiteboards, digital cameras, video cameras, and document projectors—can be terrific teaching tools. So can Web resources like blogging platforms, social media, online libraries, Google Docs, video sites like YouTube and SchoolTube, video chatting tools like Skype, and websites that provide relevant content.

These tools, when used correctly, can help further enhance your lessons, making them more digestible and sometimes more fun to your students. It's also a great way to share with the school community and parents what you're doing in class. Make a short movie with your students that relates to your science curriculum. Record a song that connects to math and match it with images to show other classes studying similar material to help them learn. Exchange blog comments or Skype with students in countries that you're studying. Technology used creatively in the classroom is not only helpful but also can be engaging.

BTW: Many of these tools can help children who normally struggle in school. For example, kids with certain reading challenges can benefit from turning the computer background black and typing in white letters, and emerging or struggling readers can benefit from interactive books that read to them and provide definitions for vocabulary words. Online math games can help students understand concepts. None of these tools can replace great teaching, but they sure can help.

The uses for technology are endless and multiplying every day. Be open to these innovations and create some of your own. If you haven't thought specifically about how you can integrate technology into your classroom, take some time to do so or speak to other teachers who have.

On the other hand, it can be challenging and frustrating if your school has little or no access to technology. With your students undoubtedly aware of the cool tools that are available, that VHS tape player and Etch A Sketch aren't going to cut it anymore. Try to find some unused computers from another classroom so you have something to start the year with. Also talk to your principal about whether your community has the resources to work as a BYOD (bring your own device) program. You can do quite a lot with some iPods and a wi-fi connection.

Do not bring computers, interactive whiteboards, or other equipment into your classroom if they don't work. And don't spend your own money on expensive items like computers, cameras, or tablets for your class. It's not fair to you.

THE INTERNET

If you're lucky, your school will be wirelessly connected and you'll have devices, such as computers and tablets, in your classroom to utilize the power of the Internet as a teaching tool. The Internet has changed the way teachers can streamline curriculum and resources into the classroom.

But the Internet can also be a dark place. Some information your students find will be incorrect or based on opinion rather than fact. Some websites are inappropriate or dangerous. If doing searches online, use search engines that are efficient, reliable, and able to find content that's age-appropriate for the grade you're teaching. Some good examples are Time for Kids (timeforkids.com), Yahoo! Kids (kids.yahoo .com), and Ask Kids (askkids.com). For teacher resources on the Web, see page 227.

Many districts block sites that they deem inappropriate for school use, but these general blocks usually restrict some pretty good sites, too. If a blocked site would be useful to your class, tell your school's technology specialist or call the district technology office and ask to have the block lifted.

BTW: Kids need to learn how to tell the difference between fiction and fact on the Internet and how to decipher between propaganda and reporting. Show your class examples of all of these and discuss—in depth relevant to their grade—what makes sites reliable or unreliable resources, so students can begin to recognize these differences on their own. You'll likely need to have a number of thoughtful discussions on how to use the Internet effectively and safely, which will help kids for years after they leave your classroom.

PREPARE, LEARN, AND TEACH

This chapter gives you a lot to think about, but once have your systems in place, you can spend most of your time during the year focused on learning and teaching—and in your first years, trust me, you'll be doing it in that order much of the time! You'll be glad you've wrangled so many moving parts before the arrival of the *real* moving parts: the students.

DURING THE SCHOOL YEAR

Once the school year begins, and you have students in your classroom every day, you'll have what seems like a million details to track—and new problems to solve every day. How do you handle a misbehaving child? How do you walk safely and orderly with your class on a field trip? What do you do with all of the supplies? How do you manage transitions from one activity to the next without losing the rhythm of the day?

You'll also be developing a relationship with an important new adult in your life: your principal. How do you build mutual trust with your principal? What do you need to know about the principal's responsibilities and personality? Should you try to be friends with him or her?

It's easy to get overwhelmed with the seemingly endless number of loose ends involved in being a teacher. This section, which covers daily life at school, provides strategies for running your class like a veteran and forging a strong relationship with your principal.

Chapter
FOUR

Working with Students

The day had finally arrived. I was so nervous I could barely breathe. I almost broke the end of the key off in the classroom door and couldn't feel my feet as I walked to pick up my first class in the foyer. I felt scared and excited at once, both proud to be starting my career and terrified of my new students. I remember finally seeing them; they looked so small and nervous. Suddenly, I felt more comfortable. We were all in the same boat.

Attending school is a common denominator among most people. Reflect upon your time as a student to inform you as a teacher. What did you like or not like? What special memories do you have that might inspire you, and what horrendous experiences do you not want to repeat? Who were the great teachers and what qualities did they possess?

Use your experience and the following tips to begin to picture how you want your classroom to function. Even if you already have a clear idea of what you want to do, this chapter can help you think about a few details you may have overlooked.

CUBBIES OR DESKS?

Everyone has an opinion about which works better, but the furniture that's available in your school will largely inform your choice. If you do have the opportunity to choose, here are some guidelines to help you make an educated decision about what will work best for you.

Cubbies are personal storage areas for students that can be made from plastic bins (like milk crates) or boxes placed in one area or around the room (or they may be built into the wall). Using the cubby system, students store their belongings, such as notebooks, journals, projects, or work they'll need during the day in their cubbies, and they work at tables, on a rug, or in a group work area. If you use cubbies, kids will be moving around the classroom more, going back and forth to their cubbies to get needed materials. One advantage is that cubbies are far easier to keep organized because they are larger and easier to see into than desks. Because of their size, more can be stored in them without compromising the material (papers getting crumpled, for example).

Cubbies also make it more difficult for kids to hide or forget things, as opposed to a desk, where a forgotten sandwich or collection of pencil stubs can get lost more easily. If you assign seats, it's easier to change these assignments if you use cubbies because students don't need to move anything from their table or desk.

If you choose desks, students keep all of their belongings inside their assigned desks. They usually work at their desks, although depending upon the activity, subject, or grouping for a specific lesson, they can sit in other parts of the classroom as well. But because the majority of their work is in their desks, they'll tend to  move around the classroom less. Desks can keep kids engaged in their table groups for longer periods of time without getting up from their seats, but this can be both a positive or a negative. Kids can get tired of sitting at their desks "all day," so if you use desks it's a good idea to build in time for them to move around.

No matter which you use, cubbies or desks can become absolutely filthy. You'd be surprised what kids store in there. Some of them are pack rats, keeping old candy wrappers, crumpled-up pieces of paper, dirty tissues, wet socks, half-chewed gum, and old food. It can get nasty, like a lab experiment gone wrong. The stench can be worse than a garbage dump, and the mess can create an eyesore in your classroom that any observer will notice, especially your students. I've been guilty of allowing this, and I learned the hard way to do a better job of checking on cubbies when my principal came into my class and reprimanded an especially messy student, then looked my way as if to ask how I missed it.

BTW: If you're not sure which system will work better for you, find out what other teachers do in your school and ask them why they use it. It's also good to know if one system is frowned upon in your school. If it is, find out why.

To keep messes like this under control, direct the kids to clean out their personal storage areas at least once every two weeks, or better yet, select a day during each week when they clean and organize their classroom space. Desks and cubbies can get so dirty you'll practically want to hose them out, so the more often they're cleaned, the better.

> **BTW:** Keep a collection of bath mats in the classroom. If a student wants to work on the floor alone or with others instead of at a desk or table, she'll have an impromptu working area that's comfortable (if you don't have a classroom rug or it's occupied). You'll want to wash those bath mats every month or so.

SEAT ASSIGNMENTS

You don't know the kids yet, so you're not going to be able to make fully informed seat assignments right off the bat. Still, don't wait until students are in the room. Do your best to assign seats before the first day of school that mix the class heterogeneously (diverse in all ways) using what you do know about your students, like gender, age, and information about specific learning needs if they have an IEP. Talk to other teachers who taught any of your students the year before. Who do the kids work well with? Find out who are, or aren't, their friends, so you know who you can encourage to sit together and who should be kept separate until you have a better command of the class. If you're teaching kindergarten and you have little information about your incoming students, do your best to mix genders, because that might be the only information you receive before the first day of school.

Make name cards that designate seats for the first day. It'll give all the kids a sense of belonging. They'll know they're expected. Let them decorate their name card as an assignment the first day of school. You might want to keep backup seat cards for the perfectionist who hates his first pass at decorating and wants to start over.

If you notice a seat assignment that's not working—for example if kids are talking too much or already arguing or fighting—don't be afraid to make a change, even more than once. Some classes can be a bigger struggle than others, but you *can* find a combination that works—at least for a little while. Don't give up.

No matter if the seat assignments are working or not, change them every three to six weeks. Don't leave students in a seat or table group for too long, even if they're working together well. Provide them the opportunity to learn from, and teach, other students and also to get a different perspective of the class. Plus, this change gives you a chance to observe students with all of their peers. Don't let the room become stagnant.

> **An upper-grade colleague of mine never assigned seats, but rather used a group of tables and a large rug area where all of the students could work. The only areas in the classroom that were labeled with their names were the cubbies, where they could place their belongings, and a hook where they could hang their backpacks and jackets. Students had the freedom to work in different areas and with different peers every day, which means they had the opportunity to learn from different peers. Although many teachers do not have the control of their class to manage such a loosely organized seating system, for her free-flowing style of teaching, it worked great and was effective.**

Once you get to know your students, mix them up on the basis of skill levels—whether it's in math, language arts, communication, or other areas—so kids can learn from each other, keeping that heterogeneous mix. You can also mix personalities. You don't want all of the loud kids at the same table, for example.

MANAGING SCHOOL SUPPLIES

Depending on where you teach, you may start the year with a plethora of supplies such as pencils, crayons, markers, glue, staples, paper, and more, or you'll be handed a few dictionaries and a box of old pencils and find yourself hitting a discount store to get the rest of what you need (if the latter is true, save those receipts for tax filing if your state offers deductibles for supplies you purchase!).

Managing in the First Days

In addition to whatever the school contributes and you buy on your own, you're likely to receive supplies from students, families, friends, other teachers, and possibly local businesses. Regardless of where the supplies come from, it can be overwhelming trying to organize all of these items during the first days of school while also trying to get to know your new students, talk to parents, and possibly deal with an entirely new school and career.

Here's a way to cope: Find three or four plastic or cardboard boxes or crates and put them against a wall. Until you can find the time to organize or distribute everything, put all the supplies in these boxes so they're out of the way and not strewn across the classroom floor or weighing down your students' backpacks. If kids have brought supplies that are for their use only, like a collection of special pencils, have them keep them in their desk or cubby. Deal with the other supplies later, when you have time to think clearly.

BTW: A good way to get the supplies you want and need without breaking into your own pocket (too much) is to ask for them in your First Day of School Note Home (see page 156). Your school or grade level may already have an annual list in place. However, be sensitive to your community's ability to afford school supplies, and try to be aware of which families in your class are unable to donate and which are simply forgetful. If you cannot figure out who is who, ask another teacher or even the office staff about the family.

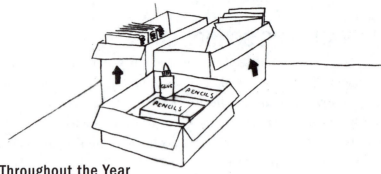

Managing Throughout the Year

Some teachers prefer to have students manage their own supplies, keeping everything in their cubbies or desks, while others use a community approach in which students borrow pencils and other materials from a central supply as needed, then return them when they're finished. I prefer the community system with the younger grades, partly because learning about sharing is often included in the curriculum. I usually let upper-grade kids manage their own supplies so they can exercise a sense of independence and responsibility. As with most systems you implement in your class, you can change it if it isn't working. You can even mix the two systems: let each table or desk cluster manage their own supplies as a group. That can be the best of both worlds.

BTW: Stockpile as many boxes of tissue as you can. Kids will be coughing and sneezing their way through the year. It can get pretty gross when colds and flus are passing through your classroom and school. Place a box of tissues in every corner. Having hand sanitizer in the classroom is a good idea, too.

If you go with the community approach, divide the supplies into two groups—those that your students will need regularly (like pencils, erasers, and crayons) and those they'll need only for certain projects (like scissors, glue, and markers)—and make sure the commonly needed supplies are readily available. Put those out in small plastic containers or old coffee cans in a few different community locations or on each table or cluster of desks. You can store the less-frequently needed materials in a (still accessible but) more out-of-the way area to save space.

> **Teachers invent systems to keep track of materials and tools in the classroom. One second-grade teacher had a few different systems to keep tools, such as scissors, glue, pencil sharpeners, and staplers, organized. Using a shelf in the middle of her classroom, she traced the outline of each supply with a black marker. If, at the end of the day, one was missing, she asked the class to find and return it. There was no questioning about how many staplers there were or where they were supposed to be. She used the same system with glue sticks. The basket was outlined on the shelf, and the number of glue sticks that were supposed to be in the basket was labeled on the front. She had a student count how many were there at the end of each day.**

Whether you use the community supply system or have kids manage their own supplies, you can use the system as a way to teach independence and responsibility—a far more important lesson than not to lose pencils. Kids will see how they can learn to take care of themselves and get what they need, as well as how to share with others and respect each other's needs, which will help them for the rest of their lives.

Managing Unwanted Donations

Sometimes, parents bring in items right when you need them, sometimes before you even think to ask. Even when you're brought random items, most can be recycled into material used for art projects. Old soccer balls can be cut up and cloth of all kinds can be saved and used. There's no end to the tidbits that can enhance a collage or diorama. But only accept donations of items you're going to use. If you're offered something you can't use, then respectfully and firmly say no thank you. Some families seem to think their child's classroom is a dumping ground for the things that they don't want anymore, like a cast-off fish tank, old bean bags, torn stuffed animals, or even smelly shoes—although I'd use the laces for something! The point is: If you don't want fish in the classroom, don't take the fish tank.

If you need something specific for a class project, such as cardboard boxes or egg cartons, don't be shy about asking the families of students for them. With any luck, someone will come through. If not, keep asking, or try local businesses or community members.

Collect the random donations that can be used for art projects—like buttons, pieces of fabric, and other odds and ends—in a bag (I used an old doctor's bag) and call it The Magic Art Bag or something similar, where all of these items live and can easily be found.

IS RAISING HANDS TOO OLD-FASHIONED?

I don't think so. There are countless ways for people in groups to indicate they have something to say, but the most commonly used signal is to raise a hand. A teacher's goal is to encourage everyone to feel supported in group discussion so they'll be willing to take a risk and contribute—without interrupting each other. The way you manage hand raising in the class can play an important role in the tone of your discussion and the comfort level of your students.

Implement hand raising on day one. Model it for your students and have them practice it over and over again. It may sound like overkill—after all, it's just hand raising—but don't expect them to learn it from day one, even if they have been raising their hand for the past five years of school. They'll need reminders and practice.

If your students raise their hands to share, it's your duty to pick someone. This can become competitive, with students moaning for you to choose them, swaying back and forth like boats lost at sea, trying to get

BTW: For younger students, it can be fun to play around with the concept. For example, instead of just raising their hand when they have something to share, tell them to raise a hand and touch their nose or their ear. Maybe they can rub their belly and raise their hand at the same time. This helps them further focus themselves and keeps their hands out of trouble (like using them to hit or push another student because they want to be picked first). I've had students raise their feet, too, but it quickly became complicated even though it was fun, because kids were rolling all over the place. For upper-grade classes, you can use the fraction or percentage of hands raised as a quick math lesson ("There are five out of 30 hands raised. That's only $1/6$ of the class.")

your attention as they hold their breath and hyperextend their fingers to try to touch the ceiling.

Don't always pick the student who raises her hand first. Give everyone time to think, perhaps waiting 5 to 10 seconds or until at least 10 students have their hand raised, including different students than those who raised their hands for the last question. If you consistently pick the quickest responder, the students who take a longer time to think will always be left out, and eventually they'll give up. You want everyone to feel encouraged to participate.

Secondly, do not allow "talking hands." A "talking hand" is when a student moans, groans, cries, squeals, or calls out your name to get your attention. Hands should be raised quietly, no matter how exciting their answer is.

Cold-calling, when the teacher calls on someone at random and the student's hand is not raised, is a method many teachers use. Although it can encourage students to always pay attention, it can also be painful and potentially damaging. A student teacher of mine cold-called a student who was not only too shy to share his ideas but

also had a memory retrieval challenge. The student froze, looking down at his shoelaces. The student teacher waited for a while, as tears welled in the student's eyes. Finally the student teacher got the message as I motioned to him to pick someone else. Although it can be a valuable tool, cold-calling can be crushing to certain students. Know who can handle this before you use it. Otherwise you'll think you're encouraging someone to share, when in actuality, you're pushing him away.

Finally, always appreciate the effort of a student who raises a hand and gives an answer, whether the answer is right or not, so he or she will feel excited to participate the next time. You might say, "I like the way you are thinking" or "How did you come up with that? Can you explain that because I think you're close and maybe someone else can help?" Don't let a student feel bad for giving a wrong answer. Mistakes can often be the best teaching moments. Make the most of them.

Many teachers, when they want to change their system of calling on someone to share, will use a class roster (see pages 44–46) instead of asking students to raise their hands. That way students know their turn is coming up (unlike cold-calling), and they can share or pass if they like. Whatever system you use, be sure it includes everyone in the class.

I CAN'T GET THEIR ATTENTION!

They're crazy! Off the wall! Talking a mile a minute and they won't listen! Do they even know I'm here! "Heeeeeellllllllllloooooooo? I'm your teacher! Listen up!"

Every teacher has felt this way. Your time will come, too. Your class will be out of control. You could offer them pizza and chocolate cake and they still wouldn't pay attention to you. How do you get them to sit up and take notice?

When I was a student teacher, one of my supervising teachers was brilliant at developing creative lessons but struggled to control a class. She would yell, stamp her feet, and bang on tables, but nothing seemed to work. She occasionally turned the lights on and off to get attention as well. One morning, about 30 minutes before lunch, the class was especially rambunctious. She went to the lights and violently turned them on and off. As the class ignored her, she did it with more force, until the unavoidable happened: all the light bulbs in the classroom blew out. Now the class was silent and sitting in a dark room (there was only one window). They all began to laugh, and the teacher now had a much bigger problem: finding the custodian to replace all the bulbs. First of all, don't use the lights to grab students' attention. But most importantly, develop methods of capturing your students' attention quickly and effectively that can be done easily in a matter of moments.

Establish a class signal or call-and-response routine as your method to get the class's attention. Students can be writing, drawing, reading, or in the middle of almost any activity, and they don't need to put down what they're doing to show you that they're listening. I like to use the "Shave and a Haircut" jingle: I say, "Bop ba-duh bop bop," and the class responds, "Bop bop." Make one up that you like. One student teacher created a new voice command. She said, "Chocolate chip cookies!" and the class responded, "With milk!"

Simple musical instruments, such as bells, rain sticks, or drums can also get your class's attention. Rhythmic clapping routines work well, too. Use a sequence of three or four different patterns. Start the year with three basic claps that they must repeat.

Whatever call or signal you use, keep it simple, rhythmic, and recognizable. If your students must think too much to know what they're supposed to do, it'll never work. Remember, too, that the louder your voice becomes, the louder the responses will be. Some kids are screamed at regularly, so your raised voice will not be as powerful to them as a quiet, calm, but firm tone. Sometimes if just one table can hear you, that's enough. The quiet will grow and spread throughout the classroom until everyone is listening. If you have students with sensory processing issues in your class, be sure to choose a signal that is sensitive to their challenges. Finally, be sure you have something important to say when you ask your class to pay attention. If not, your class will not trust that you really need their attention the next time. If you truly believe in the importance of what you're saying, most likely your students will as well. That self-confidence will go a long way in the classroom.

BTW: When the class is getting rowdy and out of control, don't be afraid to stop everything and order a moment or two of silence. When you begin to work again, they'll be calmer and more focused. No one likes to feel out of control.

TRANSITIONS

Transitions between activities can be some of the most challenging parts of the day. They can take far longer than you expect. Whether your students have to put away their work, move from one classroom to the next, or simply change position in the classroom, it can eat up time.

Before you begin any transition, know what you want your students to do. Preplan exactly what, when, how, where, and why before you begin. What are the steps they need to take to accomplish this transition? Who needs to go where?

Then break down the directions into basic, easy-to-follow instructions. Be sure that each instruction is completed before you go on to the next step. Don't rush from one step to the next. The students who finish quickly can either wait or help out others.

For example, if you want your students to put away their work and go to the Meeting Area to share their journal entries from the morning, this is one way to do it. Tell them:

- First, please put your work in your desk and sit quietly.

- Make sure all materials that you or your tablemates were using are stored in the correct places.

- Look at the floor around your seat. Is any garbage on the floor, or have any of your personal items fallen? If so, clean them up.

Then explain what is next by referring to the schedule:

- Next, we are going to share journal entries as a whole class in the Meeting Area. You will need your journal and a pencil, so please take them out and put them on the top of your desk.

- I will dismiss one table at a time. When I see that everyone at your table is ready, I will dismiss your table to come to the Meeting Area. When you get to the Meeting Area, please wait quietly or speak in a whisper to your neighbor.

- Thank you.

Then dismiss each table one by one.

> **BTW:** It's always important to thank your class! Saying thank you shows you appreciate what they're doing and is an important lesson about showing appreciation to others, even for the most menial, simple tasks.

I know. It seems laborious and ridiculous. Believe me: Even by the fifth month of school, you'd be surprised how difficult transitions are for students to do. Some will be asking you, "What am I supposed to do?" Others will be looking at a picture book, grabbing someone's pencil, or looking out the window. Be deliberate about transitions. When mismanaged, they can eat up precious minutes and expend your energy as well.

You can also help prepare your class for transitions by writing the instructions for the transition on the board. (Alternatively, you can make a poster for transitions that you can always point to, or keep a prewritten page for your interactive whiteboard that you can easily alter for different activities.) Then have a student read instructions to the class as the rest read along silently. If some of your students have audio processing issues, this will make it far easier for them to accurately follow directions. It's also a good reading and listening activity. After a student has read the transitions out loud, have a few other kids repeat them. You'll quickly know if they're totally confused by something that you thought made perfect sense. Next time, you can reword your instructions accordingly. If your students are learning to read, this can be a great shared reading activity as well.

If you're working with small groups one after another, make a chart with the names of the group members that all can see. When it's time for groups to rotate or go to a new workstation, announce who is to go where and what they'll need. Or use an easy-to-read chart so kids can see for themselves where they're expected to go. Keep it simple and clear, and alert them before you start: "For the next hour we're going to be working in our small groups. The Blue Group will start at their desks, the Yellow Group will start at the Meeting Area, and the Green Group will read in the classroom library. After 20 minutes, we'll change activities." This lets your students know where they are going and what is next. It includes them in the lesson. If not, you'll have a number of train wrecks throughout the classroom, with students going every which way, not sure what they're doing or where they're going, and bumping into each other with their books and materials falling all over the floor.

Sylvia Ashton-Warner, an educator from New Zealand and author of the book, *Teacher,* devised an effective and fun way to let her students know it was time to clean up their materials and go to the Meeting Area. Instead of clapping her hands, turning on and off the lights, or ringing a bell, she played classical music. When the students

> heard this, they knew it was time to clean up. I adopted this method, but used more contemporary music, with a good, even rhythm, like a reggae song or something similar. My students loved it, it saved my voice, and, after three weeks, we were all singing together. After a while, I had my students vote on a cleanup song and we used that for the rest of the year. You can also have students vote on a monthly change to the song as the year progresses.

Sometimes the most challenging transition is the one at the end of the day. You want your students to write down their homework, clean up their desks, pack their backpacks, grab their jackets, stack their chairs, and come to the Meeting Area or stand at their desks. There's a lot to do. In the beginning of the year, leave at least 20 minutes to accomplish this daily routine. Have one student model it for the class, or demonstrate it yourself. Be sure to write down all of the instructions clearly.

CLASS GUIDELINES AND TONE

Do you have to be a dictator with your class in order to establish structure?

The short answer is no. Don't smile before winter vacation? Some teachers use this philosophy, but I don't believe in it. By all means, smile on the first day of school but don't be a pushover. You had a mix of teachers when you were growing up. Some were unbending and others used a much softer approach. Both ways can work, and most likely you'll settle somewhere in between. If you remember back to when you were a student, I bet the most effective teachers you had were those who exuded self-confidence. Whether they were quiet, loud, sympathetic, strict, or soft, they had a sense of themselves and trusted what they were doing. No matter what your tone is in managing classroom behavior, two factors will be key to your success: consistency and student input.

BTW: Many terms are used these days to replace the word "rules," such as norms, guidelines, and agreements, all of which communicate an important idea: We, the teacher(s) and students, agree to abide by these as a class. "Rules" imply a "top down" management system while the other terms establish a feeling that you and your students are creating these together.

Consistency

Imagine if the laws of the country changed every day. No one would know what to do. Some days it would be okay to run red lights but the next day you might get a $150 ticket. Such an environment does not promote trust or understanding.

It's the same in the classroom. Consistency helps students feel more comfortable taking risks, both academically and socially, and that helps them learn—and become more independent.

Don't implement a system or rule that you're not willing to enforce for the entire year. If you say you're going to do something, you must do it. For example, if you tell your class that everyone will return to the classroom if they don't quiet down while leaving the school to go on a field trip, be prepared to follow up. If you don't, they won't believe you next time.

Setting up guidelines in the classroom and sticking to them creates clear expectations for both you and your students. Reprimanding a student for forgetting to sign out to go to the restroom on Monday but letting the same offense slide on Tuesday doesn't send a clear message. Students will be unsure of your expectations. Inconsistency creates a classroom environment where students don't feel safe or independent. They end up not knowing what is expected of them and guessing.

Student Input

Putting up a list of prewritten rules isn't going to win over any hearts early in the year. But if you include your students in the process of establishing classroom guidelines, they'll feel emotional ownership of those rules and will be more likely to stick to them.

How is this accomplished? It isn't as challenging as starting a fire in the rain, but it does take some time.

Start by brainstorming a list together. Encourage everyone to participate, and add ideas yourself. You might want to break the class into small groups to work together, which can encourage participation and generate more ideas.

You can create general behavior guidelines as well as guidelines for working in small groups, going on field trips, watching performances, and whatever else you think will help you and your class work together. List all the ideas and vote on them, either publicly or privately, shooting for a manageable number of guidelines for your class—perhaps no more than 15 for higher grades and less for kids in kindergarten, first, or second grade. Review the final list and have everyone sign it. Sometimes it might take more than a day to compile a list of norms that everyone agrees to, but that is time well spent. When the list is ready, post it in the classroom for all to see, and keep it up for the entire year. Whenever there's a problem, refer to one of the norms.

This exercise encourages your students to be independent thinkers and to take responsibility for their own classroom. It's not, "My class has strict rules," but rather, "In my class we agreed to these norms together." By including them in the process

BTW: Your first priority is to keep all of your students safe, both physically and emotionally. Never forget that. I used to tell my upper-grade students that our class was a democratic dictatorship. "We all get a say, but if there's a fire drill or someone is in danger, I make the call."

you will demonstrate self-confidence which also creates trust, unlike a top-down rules scenario. See below for a list of commonly brainstormed classroom guidelines.

Teachers, like students, should review classroom guidelines. Once a month, I review the norms of the class. Are they working? Are they current? Does anything need to be added or removed? Making changes keeps

Sample Class Guidelines

Our Class Guidelines

No hitting

Raise your hand when you have something to say

Listen to others (don't interrupt)

Respect everyone's personal property

Respect everyone's space

No spitting

No pulling hair

No throwing objects in the room

Use kind words

Clean up after yourself

Don't make other people feel bad on purpose

Don't talk behind someone else's back

Share

the guidelines fresh. With younger kids, I like to review the rules at the end of the day. This can be a great exercise, especially at the beginning of the year. One colleague I had would discuss the rules before dismissal and ask kids which norms or guidelines they had successfully followed and how, and which ones were more of a challenge that day.

If you are working with older kids, you can have them frame the guidelines more positively. For example, instead of "No spitting," use "Keep saliva in your mouth." Or instead of "No pulling hair," you can say "Keep your hands to yourself."

REWARD SYSTEMS

It's a good idea to let your class know when they're doing something you like. Compliment them when they behave in a way you want to support, or reinforce certain behaviors using a chart. On the chart, award points, stars, hearts, smiley faces, lightning bolts, or anything else to signify the accomplishment. Behaviors you might want to reward include:

- Your class lines up quickly.
- They're an especially attentive audience at a school performance.
- They read while riding the school bus or public transportation on a field trip.
- They play hard during physical education and demonstrate sportsmanship by cheering each other on.

Make it fun. After a while, your students will tell you when the class should receive points or stickers. I like to use points. Choose a number of points that the class needs to reach to receive a reward. The number must be both realistic yet not too easy to reach, so it takes some focus and effort. When that happens, you can throw a small party, watch a movie in class, hand out a healthy treat, or go to a local park to play. Do something as a group that everyone will enjoy—including you.

A former student teacher was using whole class points and it wasn't going well. She had started taking away points for individual behavior, and her class turned on those two or three kids who were "messing it up for the rest of us." Those kids were being ostracized from the group and eventually began abusing their newly found power to get the teacher to take away points. The more their classmates didn't like them, the more they used the teacher to get back at their peers, not caring about any sort of reward. It was a disaster. She learned that rewards should only be used for events or occurrences that involved the majority of the students in the classroom, and only for doing something positive. Punishing the class by taking away points for misbehavior can quickly lead to frustrated students. She stopped using points for a while and then carefully reworked the system.

Rewards are a way to acknowledge positive actions in the classroom. I like to give fewer points as the year goes on, and as some of the behaviors that earned points earlier in the year become normal and accepted, because the goal is for students to understand the intrinsic value of making positive contributions to their community, and after they leave your classroom, to the world. No one gives rewards for helping an elderly person across the street, but if you teach the benefits of being a supportive, helpful, well-meaning person in your classroom, it will encourage students to act that way for the rest of their lives.

If your students are sitting in small clusters or table groups, you can use a reward system for each group. It can be similar to your whole-class system, but at the end of every week, you reward the table that has earned the most points. It can be a great way to encourage students to work and cooperate during group projects. If I feel that a class needs some reinforcement in terms of working together and treating their tablemates well, I'll consider employing this system.

However, pitting tables in competition against each other can breed animosity. It can also be a lot of extra work to monitor the behaviors of all your tables and to award points. Be aware of how this system is affecting you and your class; if your students are thriving and you're not working too hard to manage the points, then do it.

CONSEQUENCES FOR MISBEHAVIOR

At some point, that student you've been worrying about is going to misbehave one too many times. You're going to be at the end of your rope with no patience left.

What then? At times, you'll feel like calling a taxi, and it will be a toss-up deciding who gets the cab—the student or you.

Consequences are a part of everyday life. If you drive too fast, you get a ticket. If you rob a bank, you go to jail. If you talk behind a friend's back, and the person finds out, you might lose that friend. In the classroom, consequences are meant to remind students of the agreed-upon guidelines and to teach them the behavior that is expected. Sending a child to sit in the corner of the room, facing the wall, may only humiliate him and won't stop the bad behavior.

Instead, start a list of consequences with your students. What do they come up with? What makes sense to them? Oftentimes, your idea of a consequence is less harsh than what your students can offer. Some of the consequences I have used in the past for different misbehaviors are:

- Moving the student to a different area of the classroom (if the student is fighting, teasing, or disrupting another student)

- Giving the student a "break" from class by sending him or her to another teacher's classroom for a short time (if the student is consistently misbehaving or distracting others)

- Taking away free time or choice time (if the student misuses free time)

Continue to add to your list throughout the year. Some consequences may be more effective than others. Figure out which work for your class. Try to keep the student's dignity intact. If you send someone to another classroom or revoke a privilege, don't make it into a spectacle. And don't punish yourself with a consequence for a student. For example, if you need a break from a child, but you tell her she needs to spend recess in the classroom with you, you won't get a break. The two of you will stare at each other, fuming.

When a student is misbehaving or not doing what he's supposed to do, ask the student what he thinks the consequence should be. Use the list of consequences you came up with, and come to an agreement. You'll find that most of the time, kids know what they've done and they have a good idea of what is a meaningful and appropriate consequence. (If the student doesn't offer any ideas or says he doesn't deserve any consequences, you might need to exercise some judgment and come up with consequences on your own.) Being open to discussing consequences doesn't mean you're a pushover. It means your students are taking on responsibility. You can be strict and make the discussion an expectation.

Sometimes, when students are having a conflict, all you want to do is get them to talk to each other to resolve their differences. During my second year teaching, I observed a fellow teacher, who taught first grade, resolving a disagreement between two students. But instead of talking through the problem, he sent them to the Complaint Corner. I watched the students as they read the "I-message" script that was posted there, which helped them resolve their conflict and communicate effectively.

The student who got to speak first said something like: "I don't like it when you _____. It makes me feel _____. Next time, please _____ instead."

The student who was listening held a card that read: "Please listen to your partner and answer honestly."

Then they switched. This script encouraged the students to communicate. The student who felt he was the brunt of the abusive behavior led the way. I thought this was a great idea and wrote the I-message script on a piece of chart paper and posted it in the corner of my room. I also called it the Complaint Corner. I'd send students there to resolve a conflict through open communication and self-expression. I found that most of the time students were able to resolve their differences peacefully and independently.

BTW: If a kid makes an honest mistake, such as dropping a tray of math manipulatives, punishing him won't do anything but make him nervous the next time he carries something across the classroom. We all make mistakes. If a student spills some water or drops a cup of paint, the first thing I usually say is, "Do you need help cleaning that up?" His face, usually filled with fear, relaxes as he hears my response. What's the big deal? By losing your cool, you can easily make something into a bigger problem than it really is.

Empathize

If you have a student who's acting out, try to find out what's bothering the student or provoking her to act up in class. Take the time to have a one-on-one conversation using specific questions. "Is there someone in class who is making your day a little more difficult?" "How was your evening last night?" "Did you eat a good breakfast or did your sister steal it again?" "Did something happen that made coming to school a little more difficult?" It can be helpful to use humor as well. Then ask her what happened. Often just asking what's up and listening to the answer can be the quickest road to resolving a classroom conflict. You're reaching out to your students to let them express themselves. This feels good to anyone at any time.

Behavior Contract

Sometimes a contract—a behavior agreement between you, your student, and possibly a parent or parents—is a great way to encourage responsibility on the part of the student. All people involved help write the contract, making sure the behavior is clearly explained and attainable. If a contract is unrealistic, the student will never be able to keep his or her part of the agreement. Besides realistic, make the contract positive, confidential, and derived from the ideas of the student. It should be something that you all want in terms of behavior.

For example, if a student struggles with speaking out of turn during meeting times, the student might agree to raise a hand when he wants to share an idea during Morning Meeting every day this week. This is realistic because it's not asking too much of the student (but it's still addressing the issue); it's positive because it talks about what you want rather than what you *don't* want; and, presumably, it's something both you and your student want. Asking a student to simply never speak out of turn is unrealistic and focuses on the negative behavior instead of the behavior you want.

How do you know if a student is a good candidate for a behavior agreement? There's one surefire way to find out: Try it! A student you believe has the capability to talk with you about goals and how to reach them is an excellent candidate for a behavior contract. And to me, that includes all my students. All students can be helped to understand that expectations are high for them, whether they are academic or behavior-driven. Keep the bar high for everyone who ever enters your classroom.

The class guidelines, in effect, are a behavior contract for the entire class. Check out page 122 for a sample behavior contract.

BTW: If you're up to the challenge and feeling confident, find out if something you're doing is inadvertently hurting feelings or making the child feel uncomfortable. If so, it can help the student feel more confident if you write up a behavior contract for yourself, too, and have the student sign it along with you. In a week, check to see if the two of you are making strides toward your goals.

Behavior Modifications (B-Mods)

Behavior charts, also known as behavior modifications, "Behavior Mods," or "B-Mods," are used to monitor a student's behavior during a certain part of the school day when she is struggling and encourage her to change that behavior. You can make it a part of a behavior contract. Write up the agreement so the desired behavior is observable and measurable. Asking the student to "be good" is vague, not measurable, and setting the student up for failure.

For example, if a student often interrupts during Morning Meeting, agree upon a desired behavior for that time, like raising a hand when she wants to share. Every meeting this mutually agreed-upon goal is achieved, make some sort of mark or check on the modification chart the two of you have created. If she meets the goal five times, provide some sort of reward, like 10 minutes of free reading or an extra responsibility. Focusing on the behavior you want to see rather than harping on the one you're trying to eliminate is the key to success. Afterward, get the student to mark it on her own, thereby taking responsibility for her behavior and improvement. She will become more independent by self-monitoring her actions. Eventually, you can remove the B-Mod as the student begins to see the intrinsic benefits of changing her behavior on her own.

Feedback given to a kid should be student-specific and focused on the behavior, not the student. For example, if Ixchel is writing on a neighbor's paper, you can say, "Ixchel, please write on your own paper," which is about the action, not the child. Don't say, "Ixchel, what are you doing? Why are you writing on his paper?" This reprimands Ixchel for her poor decision, most likely making her feel bad. Instead of yelling or criticizing, addressing the action and encouraging different behavior might be more effective in helping her change.

BTW: Some teachers use sarcasm, such as "nice one," "good job," or "that was some smart thinking" when they obviously mean the exact opposite. But many children have trouble understanding sarcasm, which can be both humiliating and send the entirely wrong message. Also, sarcasm can be really hurtful when it is understood. To make sure you're being as sensitive as possible with your students, avoid using sarcasm at any time, even with students who seem like they can handle it. You just can't predict how it will be taken.

Like behavior contracts, B-Mods should be kept private. Trust is paramount to changing behavior. Some children are mortified by just a frown in their direction. No one wants to feel embarrassed or labeled. Humiliation provides short-term benefits at best and makes no one feel better about themselves. Finally: If the B-Mod doesn't appear to be effective after a period of time, modify it. Keep making adjustments until you find something that works.

See page 122 for a sample B-Mod chart.

COMMUNITY BUILDING

Building a supportive community, where everyone feels welcome and safe to learn, is one of the most important things you can do as a teacher. There are countless ways to build community in the classroom. Some of it happens naturally as you all work together and go through many positive and more difficult experiences throughout the year. There are also things you can do to hurry along this process. An important but simple way is to generate class norms or guidelines together as a class (see page 109). Other simple ideas include playing name games (introduce the person next to you to the class) and doing a mystery fact list with the class, where kids secretly write down a special skill they have and others guess who has that skill.

Another way to build community is to encourage kids to express their emotions. Put a large cereal box (or something similar) in your classroom and print "The Feelings Box" on the side, and tell students they can anonymously write on a slip of paper how they are feeling or how a certain event made them feel ("I am mad at my dad because he didn't let me go to the park," "I'm sad because my grandma is sick," "I'm upset because my best friend in class is being mean to me"). The simple act of writing down the feelings can help kids feel better and build a sense of

Sample Behavior Contract

November 2

Sandy Jones agrees to raise her hand when she wants to share an idea during Morning Meeting this week and will wait to be called on before sharing.

Signed:

_____   _____   _____

Sandy Jones   Sandy Jones's Teacher   Sandy Jones's Parent

Sample Behavior Modification Chart

Sandy's Behavior Chart

Each day that Sandy speaks during Morning Meeting only after being called on, she will receive a checkmark on this chart. For every five checkmarks, she receives 15 minutes of extra free reading time (the reward she chose).

	Monday	Tuesday	Wednesday	Thursday	Friday
Jan 7–11	✔	✔			
Jan 14–18					
Jan 21–25					
Jan 28–Feb 1					
Feb 4–8					

confidence and camaraderie in your class, but at some point, you can also choose a few of the feelings from the box to discuss, anonymously, with the class. You might lead a discussion about how to resolve a situation if the note raises one, or you can ask kids in class to express empathy toward the person. Be sure the note's author remains anonymous; don't pick any notes that would give away who wrote them.

I like to do a Truth Circle every Friday, where all the students have a chance to say something that is going well for them and something that is more challenging. It's a time for kids to share and get to know each other. With younger kids, I did a Weather Report, where one morning per week we would go in a circle and kids could share how they were feeling by describing their personal weather (sunny, rainy, partly cloudy, etc.). It was an effective means for kids to begin feeling comfortable expressing feelings. Be sure to do what is comfortable for you. It's important for kids to feel safe enough to express what is going on in their lives. It is part of who they are and affects how they learn.

Before doing any of these activities, you must create guidelines for all of the class, including you, to follow, or no one will share because they fear being teased or not being taken seriously. Guidelines create trust, which is paramount to students feeling comfortable to express their feelings. Sometimes serious issues might come up. If they do and they seem a little too personal for you to deal with, speak to your school social worker. You're not a therapist, so resolving these problems is not your job.

CELEBRATE YOUR STUDENTS' WORK

Let your students feel like celebrities! Go beyond displaying their work on bulletin boards by throwing events to show how proud you are of them and their accomplishments. For example, have a publishing party, where kids read their completed works to parents and students from other classes.

Or create a class museum for parents and other students to visit. Publish a book of student poems to give out to parents and have a poetry reading. You can also read a poem from the book each morning. How about having your students perform a simple skit, play, or choral song for the school or in a public venue like a mall or government building?

Any of these ideas will make your students feel great, provide an opportunity for parents to be involved in their child's class as an observer or helper, and make you and your students more visible in your school community. Events make the school look great, and by organizing them, you're adding to the general energy of the campus.

TEACHING WHOLE CLASS, SMALL GROUPS, AND ONE-ON-ONE

Did you ever visit a classroom where the teacher was standing at the front of the room as students fell asleep on their books? You can avoid being that teacher by mixing it up. Teach the whole class when it's appropriate, but break up into small groups frequently to take advantage of the lower student-to-teacher ratio for more impact during your lessons. Both can be effective for different activities. And while it obviously takes a lot more of your time and considerable planning ahead, I try to find time to conference with kids one-on-one to go over their individual work, projects, or a point with which they are struggling.

Whole Class

When you address your entire class at once, it's easy for some students to fall between the cracks, yawning their way through whatever you're trying to teach. Half your class thinks it's important, but other kids are drawing, picking their nose, or staring out the window. And it's very hard to assess your students' understanding while standing at the front of the class unless you break into small group activities soon after.

When you teach to your entire class, whether you have 15 or 35 students, keep these key concepts in mind.

- Be sure you can see the whole class. Eye contact when speaking to your entire group is important. You don't want three kids hiding in the back or side of the room.

- Don't go on forever. Many new teachers plan lessons where they stand in the front of their class talking for way, way too long. You'll need to be the judge of what is too long, but remember, at the beginning of the year, students' attention spans will be far shorter. Help them build it up.

- If you're going to have kids addressing the whole class, have them participate in small-group discussions first, or even one-on-one partner discussions while sitting next to each other, then report back to the whole class. Asking students to raise their hand and speak in front of the entire class can be intimidating, but if you have them discuss your question or idea in small groups before they respond in front of the class, it can boost their confidence because they will have already developed the idea they want to share.

Small Groups

Teaching small groups is fun and effective. You get to know the kids better in this more intimate situation, and you can communicate a lot more information to them in a short period of time compared to working with the whole class. It's also far easier to assess understanding—and who needs help and who needs more of a challenge—when teaching in small groups because you have fewer kids to attend to at that moment. It's easier to encourage participation and conversation and to be more involved in what the students are thinking or trying to figure out. Fifteen minutes with a small group can make a world of difference, as opposed to even twice that time with an entire class.

You can divide up the groups by making them homogeneous—students who have similar skills or characteristics—or heterogeneous—students whose skills and abilities are diverse. But how do you know what to do for which subjects?

I use homogeneous skill groups for math, reading, spelling, and sometimes writing. The students in class are typically on very different ability levels, so grouping kids with similar skills together is a convenient way to differentiate instruction for those groups. I use heterogeneous groups for subjects such as social studies and science, where all kids need to learn similar information and their diverse skill sets can help them teach each other. But this can be flexed. I regularly change up groups depending on what will be the most effective way for a specific lesson.

These groups are a starting point and are meant to be flexible. Don't be afraid to change groups. If a student seems like he needs to change a group for academic or social reasons, don't hesitate. Students, like all of us, change as time goes on.

But what do the other kids do while you're working with a small group? The rest of the class can be working on independent work, or you can assign various problems to different groups and have them work independently as you make your way around the classroom.

> **BTW:** If you name homogenous groups by level, such as A, B, C, and D, or 1, 2, 3, and 4, students are going to figure out if they are in a "lower" or a "higher" group. This will lead to questions like "Why can't I be in the smart group?" or "Why am I in the stupid group?" Instead, use innocuous names, like colors, that have nothing to do with levels or numbers, or better yet, have the groups name themselves. Do the same with heterogeneous groups sometimes, too. Let them pick a name they'll be proud of.

One-on-One

During an independent work time, silent reading, or even during recess if a student is available and willing, make time to conference with students one-on-one. Use this time to review concepts or go over specifics of their work. A one-on-one conference can be as short as two minutes but can still be quite valuable: Even if you have nothing academic to discuss (though you almost always do), you can use this time to see how students are feeling about school, if they feel behind, or if they have any interpersonal issues—for example, with another student—that are concerning them.

If you're using one-on-one conferences to go over a concept with each child, be sure to use a class roster to make sure you don't miss anyone.

> **BTW:** When conferencing with a student, face the class so you can see everyone else. Yes, you will be multitasking a little, but if something happens, like a fight breaking out or someone making an unannounced visit to your class, you want to be aware of what is happening and ready to address it.

GETTING YOUR CLASS INTO THE WORLD: TIPS FOR FIELD TRIPS

A number of things need to be taken care of before you leave for a field trip. Here is a list of ideas to start with (you should be able to answer "yes" to all these questions):

- Do you have all of your permission slips?
- Have you organized the transportation to and from the site? (If you're using a private bus company, be sure to contact them the day before the trip to confirm.)
- Did you contact the site administrator (by email if you can, so you have a record of the confirmation) to confirm your arrival?
- If needed, do you have snacks for your students?
- Is there a place where your class can eat lunch?
- Will water be available, or do students need to bring their own?
- If it's going to be a longer trip, do your students have materials to keep themselves occupied, like books or journals and a pencil?
- Do you have a copy of the class roster with each student's family and emergency contact information?
- Do you have extra supplies like pencils and tissues?
- Do you know what first-aid you are allowed to bring or administer?

Get through this list at least the day before you depart to leave yourself room to make last-minute changes or get things done!

Plan for the Season

When planning a field trip, be sure to think about the season. If you live in a cold climate, you might want to plan a number of indoor trips for the winter months. If the climate in your area changes a lot with the seasons, different class excursions offer different educational value depending upon when you go. For example, a nature center might provide fewer teaching moments for your curriculum about leaves if you go midwinter in a cold climate than if you go in the fall or spring. I take my class to a local park to do community service cleanup. When we go in the winter, there's less to do, but in the fall and spring, it's nonstop participation.

> I had carefully planned a field trip to the zoo in springtime for my first-grade class. We were close to finishing our unit studying animals, and this was going to be a culminating experience. When we arrived at the zoo I realized I had made a mistake. I forgot what animals do in the spring—mate. As we were watching two chimpanzees mate, one of my students looked at me and said, "Mr. K, it seems like they like each other." Next year we went to the zoo in the fall.

Traveling with Your Class

A number of years ago I saw a TV commercial for a bank. It showed a young, smartly dressed teacher in a deserted natural history museum walking her class past the skeleton of a dinosaur. All the students were holding hands, following one after another, looking like they were practicing for the ballet. That is a far cry from reality. More likely, you'll be plowing your way down a crowded street, trying to pull your class through a hectic entranceway, or organizing them on a school bus. With 20 to 30 kids, that can be a handful. However, a few tricks can make traveling with your class easier.

- **Choose one line or two.** One line can be long, depending upon your class size, but your students might tend to focus more on walking. In two lines, they walk with a partner and the line is shorter, though they might get distracted by chatting or fighting with each other.

- **Know where the restrooms are.** Whether you're traveling across the school yard or across town, always know where the restrooms are en route—or if there aren't any at all, plan ahead. You don't want to be stuck with a kid jumping up and down, about to pee his pants, when you're 10 minutes from any toilet.

- **Assign jobs to students.** Give kids the roles of line leaders and back-of-the line leaders (who make sure everyone is walking together and no one has fallen off the pace of the class) when you walk as a class. They will help you keep the line organized and keep your class walking together.

- **Monitor the line.** It's a myth that the teacher must walk in front of the line. When she does, she cannot see that four kids in the back of the line are dragging 100 yards behind, two kids are fighting, and one stopped to tie her shoe, which can take a while for some. When the teacher arrives at her destination with her class, she is surprised that only half the class is there. Instead, stroll up and down the line, watching your class walk, making sure everyone is staying together, and helping anyone with untied shoes, spilled lunch boxes, broken umbrellas, and the like. You can talk to students and monitor your class instead of being stuck at the front of the line, trying to walk backward and yelling at the kids in the back of the line to hurry up. If you have parents helping on the trip, you can have them help you monitor the line, too.

> **BTW:** Choosing partners can be a difficult process. If you let students pick their own buddies, they feel a sense of independence but feelings can be hurt. Mixing up genders and friends is a natural way to integrate your class on a field trip. Once you assign partners, make them stay together. If you allow some kids to make changes, no one will listen to you the next time around.

- **Plan to stop.** Pick periodic destinations along your traveling route, such as exit signs, stop signs, stores, or telephone poles, and direct the class to stop there. When the front of the line stops and everyone is together, pick the next destination: "Please walk ahead four parking meters and stop."

- **Count them.** Keep counting your class as you travel. Walk up and down the line to be sure everyone is there. If your class is walking in pairs, it's that much easier because you can count your class by twos.

It may sound silly, but safe, efficient line-walking takes a lot of practice, and no location is better to work out the kinks of the system than the hallway or grounds of your school. Walk up and down the hallway, using stopping points like fire extinguishers, drinking fountains, and classroom doors. Before you go on a field trip, whether it's a daylong trip or a walk around the neighborhood, be sure you have complete control of your class. You don't want to run into unforeseen problems (oh, they'll come up, don't worry) when you're in public. Try to have everything under as much manageable control as you can.

A word about the general public: People may offer help if a kid drops a backpack, a shoe falls off, or someone is straggling way behind. They're almost certainly just trying to be helpful, but you should always be cautious anyway, and trust only your assigned class volunteers. You never know what a seemingly helpful person's intentions are. Your responsibility is to keep your students safe.

Finally, don't forget to count your students before you leave the school, during your excursion, and again before you leave the site to return to school. (I know I said it before but it is worth saying again!) That way you can make sure nobody is left behind.

DID YOU TALK TO ALL OF YOUR STUDENTS TODAY?

You're probably going to think about your students nonstop, day and night, especially in your first few years in the classroom. Being an elementary school teacher is all-encompassing, but that doesn't necessarily mean you're paying equal attention to all of your students.

A colleague and I were talking about our students after school one winter afternoon. He was complaining that two kids in his class with behavior problems were taking up all of his energy. Other students in the class were complaining that he didn't spend enough time with them. He felt awful; he was ignoring some of the students who were working really hard and he hadn't even known it. After this he made a point of starting each day speaking with a different student to try to spread out his time with his students more evenly.

One way to be sure you're connecting with each and every student is to write down their names after they leave for the day. The three to five kids who are at the bottom of your list—or the few kids you didn't remember—are probably the ones who could use some more of your attention. Make a plan for seeking out these kids and spending some time with them first thing the next morning. Keep doing this exercise, and be aware of how the list changes. If the same kids are always in the middle of the list, spend some extra one-on-one time with them as well. No one wants to be ignored, especially by the teacher. This will help you be sure that you spend time with everyone in class, and your students will notice and appreciate the attention.

WHEN THE RUBBER HITS THE ROAD, BE FLEXIBLE

This chapter is full of advice, from choosing between cubbies and desks to managing behavior and traveling with your class. But maybe the most important takeaway of all is that you'll need to be flexible. Your students and you are human beings, and sometimes your plans don't work out the way you expect. Maybe that B-Mod doesn't modify anything, or that field trip turns out to be a disaster. When these things happen, try to stay cool and be aware of yourself—how you sound, what you're saying, how you look—and be sure it's true to who you are. Believe in yourself. Self-awareness and self-confidence are worth years of experience, and if you can find them early on, they will help you every day.

Chapter

FIVE

Working with Your Principal

When you join a school as a new teacher, veterans are likely to offer dire advice and stories about your principal:

- "Don't bother her on Monday, unless it's life threatening, like you're being chased down the hall by a parent or a child is being taken to the emergency room. Save it until later in the week."

- "She was the best teacher you've ever seen and she's an even better principal. She's the reason the school runs so well. And she lets you know it."

- "When you hear his voice down the hallway, quietly close your door so he doesn't come in."

- "He works so hard helping his teachers during the day I think he stays all night to get all of his paperwork completed."

- "She doesn't have fangs that I can see—unless it's testing season."

More stories circulate throughout schools about principals than bad food served in cafeterias. The rumors that they're overworked, stressed, and generally too busy to deal with you can be true, but not always.

Principals, like every boss, come with different histories and personalities. There's the overworked, exhausted, stressed-out principal. Then there's the relaxed, "nothing will ever ruffle my feathers" principal. You may be familiar from your own school days with the "nothing can stop our school, we are the best!" motivational speaker type of principal. There's the quiet but frightening principal, who the entire school fearfully notices when he raises an eyebrow. There are principals who are frantic while others could defuse a bomb without losing a drop of sweat.

Some will be present in their teachers' everyday work life and others are rarely seen.

The fear most people carry of their bosses is usually unnecessary and always counterproductive. No one teaches well while afraid. Fear results in overly cautious rather than passionate teaching, which isn't good for you, your students, or anyone else.

Always keep in mind that the job of a principal is a tough one. The responsibilities are enormous and the amount of communication needed in one day is overwhelming. It's like organizing a parade, every day of the week. And as the climate in education continues to be high pressure and stressful, more and more weight is placed upon the shoulders of principals.

But even if most principals are overworked, that doesn't mean they can't be a resource for you. I've been fortunate to have worked with a group of inspired principals who taught me a lot about teaching, how schools function, and how best to work with them. Your principal can be an incredible ally, a teacher, an inspiration, and a terrific leader, even if she does reveal her fangs sometimes (don't we all?). Whether you like your principal or not, building a strong, professional relationship with her will benefit you both.

TRY TO SOLVE THE PROBLEM ON YOUR OWN

If you have a problem in your classroom—an out-of-control child, a parent who won't stop bothering you, or a struggle with part of the curriculum—the principal can be a good person to talk to. But the most important step for you to take before you approach a busy principal is to try to remedy the situation yourself. Don't hide issues from your principal, but use other resources first. Try talking with colleagues or, if it's a problem with a child or a family, find out who worked with them the year before.

> It was my first year teaching and I was struggling with a misbehaving student. I tried a number of different ideas to improve his in-class behavior, including preferential seating, carefully selected work groups, independent work periods, and time in another classroom. Nothing seemed to work. He came to class a ball of unbridled angry energy and maintained that disposition throughout the day. One afternoon, after an especially difficult day, I went to ask my principal for help. I was about to knock on her door when someone tapped me on the back. It was my (invaluable) assigned mentor. She said, "Whatever that problem is, the first thing she is going to ask is what have you done to try to solve it." I said, "I've tried a list of strategies." "Good," she responded. "The second thing she is going to ask is who you have asked for help." I hadn't asked a soul. After an uncomfortable moment of silence, she continued. "Then she is going to kick you out of there, with a smile, and the next time you need her, she may ignore you, and that might be when you really need her help. Before you access the power behind that door, use your colleagues first."

If you've come to the point where you've tried a number of strategies to resolve an issue, and you've consulted with a few fellow staff members as well, *then* approach the principal. Make an appointment and let her know what you've tried and who you've asked for assistance so she can effectively help you. A principal can be a wealth of knowledge if her time is used appropriately.

Obviously, if there's an emergency, don't hesitate to inform your principal right away, even if she doesn't like to be disturbed. She is responsible for the school, and she should know about anything urgent.

PRINCIPALS NEED YOUR HELP, TOO

Although your principal may seem intimidating and omnipotent, he needs your assistance and help, too. As you get to know his daily patterns or style, think about what you could do to make his load a little lighter.

> **BTW:** Teaching is the kind of job where you learn by doing. The fear that plagues many first-year teachers is being seen as incompetent. You're new to the profession, and it's natural to feel like you don't want to mess up ever, but remember that learning from the mistakes you make is part of what will turn you into a great teacher. Your principal—who most likely was also a teacher—should know that and will likely help you learn from your mistakes.

For one thing, be reliable about doing the daily, mundane things required of you: showing up on time for school and meetings, filling out forms on time, thoughtfully writing your report cards in a timely manner, and so on.

Here are three others things you can do to help your principal (and make yourself look good in his eyes):

1. Keep Your Principal Informed

This doesn't mean banging down the door with every little question, problem, or success story. It does mean keeping her up-to-date on the original, creative aspects of your teaching, things that you have learned or want to share because you think they might help other teachers.

My principal visited my first-grade classroom one morning. As part of our study of the seasons, we were making facemasks for each season, combining the physical elements of the weather with how the season made us feel emotionally. A small group painted each seasonal mask and wrote a list of words describing each season to hang below the mask. My principal asked me to stop by her office before the end of the day. When I did, she was in the midst of a storm of chaos, but surprisingly she took a moment to let me know that she'd loved my project. She said, "If you're doing something like that—original, special, a play on the existing curriculum—please let me know. I want to know about these things so I'm informed and so when visitors come I know about special projects. Also, I was a teacher, too, and I love seeing these things. If I'm busy, just drop a note in my box or send me an email. I don't want to miss out!"

Most people only approach principals with problems; then the principals end up spending their days putting out fires. Be sure to share success stories and celebrations with them as well. They'll appreciate it.

2. Share Ideas and Opinions

You don't need to be a cheerleader, but voicing your opinion when asked and speaking up in meetings are the kind of enthusiastic participation your principal will appreciate because it helps make her life easier. Don't spend the entire year hiding out in your classroom, either. Share ideas and success stories with other staff. The ideas you share might potentially be a resource for someone else on the staff. Even if your opinion or idea conflicts with those of others, it could serve as the spark for a conversation that will lead to an improvement for the school.

3. Take on Extra Tasks

There are always a million loose ends to take care of in any school, and you can easily assist your principal a lot by pitching in to help. That could mean helping manage dismissal, lending a hand in the school yard, or absorbing a few kids from an absent teacher's class when no sub is available. People get sick, leave, don't show up, or for other reasons need help with their responsibilities. Get used to the idea of seeing what needs to be done and stepping in.

> In the class I taught one year, all of my students took the bus home every day. Some of them traveled for up to 90 minutes each way. I made it my business to walk my students to their buses to make sure they knew where they were going and that there were no problems. The drivers would inform me if any kids were misbehaving, and I would support them from my position as classroom teacher. My principal, doing a random check on the buses one afternoon, was surprised to find me helping kids get to their correct ride home. I explained that I walked my students out every afternoon to make myself seen, to make sure everything was okay with the drivers, and to ensure there were no problems. I also helped out the other kids as well. She loved it and created a position for me: Bus Coordinator. Every afternoon I made sure all of the kids got on the right bus and if the drivers had a problem they reported to me. She even offered me a small stipend that she found in her budget. Being a new teacher, I was able to get to know a majority of the kids in the school and help out by doing something I was already doing. It worked for everybody.

While it's great to help out, and your principal (and colleagues) will appreciate it, take care not to pick up too many extra responsibilities. Remember your priority is to be prepared to teach your class.

BTW: The best-case scenario is to have a strong working relationship with an effective, supportive principal. Sometimes, of course, this isn't the case. If you feel you're being treated unfairly by your principal, speak to a trusted colleague (or colleagues) to get advice for that specific situation. Maybe you're not seeing it clearly, or maybe the colleague has an idea about how to solve the problem more easily. Do everything you can to resolve it, but if all else fails, speak with your school-based teacher representative. He or she may want to arrange a meeting with your principal to talk about the differences with the rep present. This is a big step and can be potentially damaging to your relationship with your principal, so this should be your last option. If the situation doesn't change, you might have to think about looking for a new job next year.

WHAT PRINCIPALS CAN DO FOR YOU

Principals can do a lot for you. Obviously they can be mentors, helping you solve classroom and curricular problems and develop as a teacher. Usually, principals will have a lot more experience than you do. They are a resource you should tap and use to your advantage. They can provide gems of advice regarding in-class ideas and possibly how best to manage your time, energy, and priorities so you're not exhausted every day.

But one of the most valuable benefits of a supportive principal is that she will defend you in the event that you have a conflict with a parent, outside observer, or another staff member. For example, if a parent challenges you about an in-class issue, your principal will support you and serve as an intellectual bodyguard. That can go a long way.

MAKING FRIENDS WITH YOUR BOSS

Working with your principal, as with any boss, is, at its best, a collaboration. You're both aiming for the same goal, which is to create a learning environment that is inspiring, safe, challenging, and fun. It's in your principal's interest for you to do your best.

Most importantly, your principal can become a workplace friend and mentor. I've always found my relationships with my principals beneficial, even during rough times—and you'll have rough times. But if you think of your principal as an ally and take the time to get to know him or her, it will benefit both of you.

YOUR STUDENTS' FAMILIES

Although at first it can be intimidating, working with the parents of your students can be a fun and enriching part of the job. It can also be very beneficial for all three parties—you, the student, and the family—when you all work together. During your career you'll come into contact with families at many different levels of involvement, from the extra-eager parent who wants to volunteer as a full-time job to the families who never respond to correspondence. The wide-ranging benefits and challenges presented by students' families is something you'll always be adapting to.

This section provides suggestions for communicating with families, coping with unhappy parents, running successful Back to School Nights and parent-teacher conferences, and managing parent volunteers, all of which are to help encourage parent involvement.

BTW: Some of your students won't have a mom or dad present in their lives for various reasons, and it may be some other family adult that you're in touch with. When I use the words "parent" and "parents," I'm referring to nuclear parents, stepparents, foster parents, grandparents, older siblings, aunts and uncles, and all other family adults that you'll be in contact with.

Chapter SIX

The Parent-Teacher Relationship

Parents: Are they going to be nasty? Nice? Hate how you teach? Praise your every move? Hound you? Argue with you? Throw a party to thank you for your teaching? Stalk you? Send you multiple emails every night? Never show up to any meetings you schedule? Are parents really the monsters you're fearing, or the gentle helpers you're hoping for?

Okay. Time for a deep breath. Many new teachers have a lot of fear about dealing with their students' families, but keep those nightmares and fantasies in check. Most parents are supportive and just want to see their kid succeed.

The better your relationship with parents, the more effective you'll be in helping kids succeed. However uncomfortable the thought may make you, being available to parents—and extending yourself to make participation easy for them—is an important part of the job. And contrary to popular rumor, working with parents can be a satisfying, enriching aspect of your teaching career.

Getting to know the family will help you contextualize the life of the child. Just as many younger students think their teacher lives at school (I remember one first grader who was shocked to discover that I didn't sleep there), it's easy to forget that your students have a life outside of the classroom, too. Your students play sports, enjoy hobbies, and are part of extended families. Parents can help you more fully comprehend the tendencies, strengths, challenges, and needs of your students. In short, families make the job more interesting—and they can make you better at it.

It's important to realize that, for many parents, schools can be big, confusing, secretive, and possibly threatening environments. They may have no clue about what is going on. The last time they were in an elementary school could have been at least 20 years ago, and their own experiences in school vary wildly. This may cause them to come into your classroom with preconceived ideas about what an elementary school and schoolteacher should look like—ideas that might be way off base. Or they may completely avoid the school because of their own experience with education or because of obstacles in their lives. Their kids may or may not tell them what is happening in school, so communicating with you might be their only window to learn about their child's experience.

Remember that most parents are anxious about any bad news concerning their child. Be empathetic. Compassion will make you a better communicator.

Most of all, if parents feel comfortable with you, they're more likely to get involved in their child's education. With their attention and support, students will feel like their parents think school is that much more important. Consequently, the

BTW: A student in a teacher education course told me she wanted to be a teacher because she liked spending time with kids, not adults. I suggested that she rethink the idea of becoming a teacher. A large portion of the job is working with the parents, extended family members, and often other adults in your students' lives. It's great, of course, to love spending time with kids, but if you struggle with adults, the job may not be for you.

child will feel increasing enthusiasm from their families, which will make everyone's lives easier and you more effective.

WHAT YOU WANT FROM PARENTS

Positive parent-teacher relationships can vary as widely as the types of parents you'll encounter, but in general, the best relationships are ones in which the teacher and the parent both contribute to the student's intellectual and emotional development. Here are some guidelines of what hypothetically "ideal parents" would do.

- They support your good decisions and ask critical questions when they don't, thereby helping you articulate your vision.
- They respond to requested inquiries, hand in all forms and fees on time (or ask for financial assistance if needed), and make sure their kid does his homework and is as well-rested as possible.
- They read the notes you send home and respond if needed.
- If they join you on a field trip or volunteer in class, they actually help the entire group and don't focus only on their child.
- If they have a problem, they come to you to discuss it instead of yelling at you, complaining to other parents, or going directly to the principal.
- They want to know about the curriculum and information being taught in class, and they pay enough attention so they do. Even if it's academically a reach for them, they show support and a willingness to help support their child's work.
- They are aware of your role in the life of their child, and they appreciate it. This doesn't necessarily mean you'll hear from them often or they'll shower you with compliments.

But most of all, they're present to the needs of their child as well as aware of what you're teaching in class.

WHAT PARENTS WANT FROM YOU

BTW: When working with parents, remember that you're not looking for new friends. You're looking for relationships to help you do the best job you can as the child's teacher.

How can you help make parents happy? One of the most important ways is to communicate with them. Most parents want to know what is happening in the life of their child. Make it is easy for them.

You don't need to send a note home every day, but keeping parents informed about the classroom will help keep them out of your hair and help disengaged parents get involved. This can be as simple as regularly sending home copies of schoolwork, but it also includes notes home to parents that update them about activities you're doing in class and what curriculum you're covering. (See the Weekly Note Home on page 173.) Many parents will want to know exactly how you're addressing standards, testing, and other curricular objectives, so you'll want to let them know about that, too.

Finally, talk yourself (and your class) up a little bit. Let families hear about your successes. Show them how life in your classroom is exciting, interesting, and fun. They want to feel your dedication and passion. You don't need to decorate the entire classroom in balloons and streamers, but when you communicate with parents, brag about the compelling activities and projects the class is doing and the interesting moments in the curriculum. If they visit the classroom, show them cool projects so they can see for themselves. Parents who normally do not participate for a variety of reasons will be more excited to do so if their child is doing positive, interesting things.

Part of communicating is listening, too, so be sure to pay attention to their concerns and complaints. Even if you disagree with what they're saying, hear them out. Usually you can do something to smooth things over, even if you can't change their child's grade or expel the kid who is bullying her. Keep in mind that it's their kid you're working with. They're likely to be a lot more emotionally involved than you. By listening and showing empathy, you're also encouraging them to continue to participate, which helps the student.

WHAT MIGHT MAKE PARENTS UNHAPPY WITH YOU

If you're communicating with parents and you're showing passion and competency in teaching their child, why would they be unhappy? They should feel lucky to have you teaching their child! You're the perfect teacher, right?

Parents can get upset for many reasons, many of which are very rational. Does a mom think you were mean to her child? Did a child's feelings get hurt in class, and now the child feels unsafe? Did you forget to send home an assignment? Was your instruction on something ineffective in teaching a student? Be honest with yourself about why a parent is upset, and if the reason is a rational one, apologizing is a good way to start making up for your mistake or for a misunderstanding.

BTW: Remember, many parents' anger or frustration with you can be due to the fact that they're not familiar with the classroom, school processes, or the curriculum. Sometimes an emotional outburst is merely a heated request for information.

Many times, parents get upset due to an inaccurate message they're receiving from their child. Maybe the child says there is no need to study for Friday's quiz when you told the class just the opposite, or the child tells the parent that you never allow kids to ask questions during math when in fact you always encourage questions. When a parent is angry with you, first look to clear up any crossed lines of communication. Their anger may dissipate in the seconds it takes for you to explain yourself.

Sometimes, though, opinions and personalities just will clash. There are always going to be people you don't click with, and some of those people are going to be the parents of your students. They might not like you for reasons that are totally out of your control. Don't take it personally if a parent doesn't like you because you remind her of an ex-sister-in-law. Work with what is in your control to make the relationship the best it can be.

Just as you will have unique relationships with each of your students, the same goes with their parents. You have to handle each relationship differently. Do your best to be aware of how parents feel about you, and try to diffuse difficult situations before they escalate. Most times you will be able to work things out easily.

METHODS OF COMMUNICATION

Here are the four most important methods of communication:

- Email
- Class website
- Phone calls
- Notes in Homework Folders

Email

The almighty power to email has made reaching out to families infinitely easier for teachers. Mass emails to parents about field tips, lice in school, vacations, half days, homework, special events, fundraisers, and photos and stories from the classroom are easy to create and it keeps everyone informed.

Warning: Remember, what you write in an email creates a permanent record. Use email only for mass communication to the class, logistics, and other school-based information. Sensitive subjects, such as behavior or academic issues, should not be handled by email because there are so many ways to be misunderstood. Instead, make a phone call or set up a meeting to discuss these subjects. If you receive an email or note about a sensitive subject, simply respond by asking for a good time to talk on the phone or to meet face-to-face. If the parent persists, don't give in. It's always better to meet face-to-face about sensitive subjects or at least speak on the phone. Sometimes, if you insist upon a meeting, the problem dissipates.

For all school-related emailing, set up an email account that's separate from your personal email. If your school or district provides you with one, you can use that. Who wants to be reading an email about a date you're about to go on and receive an email from a grumpy parent? Your school email address is where parents email you and where you order books for your classroom and deal with other school-related issues. Your principal and fellow teachers can use this email for all school-based information.

If your school doesn't provide you with an email address, use any of the many free email services that are available (such as Gmail, Yahoo!, Hotmail, Care2, Green Geeks, and a million others) and make an address that contains your name and some combination of your grade, room number, or school. It might look something like this:

- Otis4th502@XXXXX.com
- Mr.K502@XXXXX.com
- YourTcherMrK@XXXXX.com

Create one you like that's easy to remember.

It's a good idea to set up email hours, just like office hours, so parents know when you'll check it. For example, tell parents that you periodically check email from 8 a.m.–5:30 p.m., Monday–Thursday. On Fridays, check it at 3:30 p.m. and then again on Sunday evening.

BTW: Check your school email more than you say you will. I usually check it when I get up in the morning and before I go to bed at night, no matter how late, in case there's something important I need to respond to. Parents feel cared for when they get an email back at 11 p.m. or 5:30 a.m.

Class Website

If you teach in a community where Internet access is common, you'll probably want to maintain a class website to post announcements, reminders, spelling lists, a calendar, the homework list, worksheets, and links to Web resources that families might find useful. It might even be required by your school. A website is a convenient way to keep families and older students informed, and it can really cut down on the number of messages you have to send home. If you do have a class website, be sure to update it regularly. It's frustrating for parents to go to a class website to get the weekly spelling list only to find the most recent list is from a month ago.

The best situation is if your school hosts a website with separate pages for each classroom. That way, families can access general information about the school and district, and school-wide announcements and events are kept up-to-date for you. If you need to host it on your own, you can use one of many free hosting services. Check with your principal before posting any photos of kids. It may be against the school rules.

Phone Calls

The last time I checked, I couldn't call my mechanic at nine o'clock at night. Nor could I phone my dentist, even if I had a roaring toothache. I have to wait until the morning. The same goes for a teacher.

You need space from this all-encompassing job. Although many teacher-training programs now recommend that fielding phone calls during the evening is part of the job, it shouldn't be a nightly occurrence.

You don't want to avoid communicating with parents or make it more difficult for those who want to talk with you. Just be sure to set boundaries for yourself. You need a life of your own to be a great teacher (see Chapter 10).

> **My first year of teaching, I made the mistake of returning a phone call to a parent from my home phone. She called me for the rest of the year in the evenings with little questions, leaving me voice mails asking how the day went. I asked her repeatedly to please email or wait until school hours. She ignored my requests, and finally I learned to recognize her number on my caller ID and not answer the phone when it was her. Block your phone number when making phone calls from home or your cell phone (different phone companies have different ways of doing this; check with your phone company about how you can do it).**

Even though you want to avoid evening phone calls and making calls from home, there will be times when a phone call during the evening is needed. If a parent works at a job where communication during the day isn't possible or there's a family emergency, be sure to take the time to reach out.

> **A parent needed to get in touch with me, but she had no email. She came to school frustrated and angry because I hadn't given out my home phone number. Exasperated, she began to cry. Her son was in the hospital with an asthma attack and she wanted me to know that he wasn't going to make the school performance the next day. I expressed my concern and sorrow and told her next time to call another parent in the class who had email, or better yet, call the school. If a message reaches me, I can always call her back. Her reaction was, "I wish I'd thought of that!" She felt satisfied that I had heard her concerns, and I kept my boundaries firm but friendly. (I also made an exception and checked in with her by phone a few nights that week.)**

Sometimes a phone call is needed to report an emergency (usually the office will do that), discuss a sensitive issue or incident that occurred during the day, touch base with a parent, or welcome a new family to the class. Use the school phones. You don't need to set up "phone hours" because you will use the phone infrequently.

Learn where in the school are phones that you can use with some semblance of quiet and privacy. Making a phone call from the office to a family to tell them their child was in a fight, got a black eye during

> **BTW:** I like to use school phones for daytime calls to parents because most people have caller ID. When parents recognize that it's the school calling, they usually pick up.

recess, or bombed the most recent math assessment while the staff is having lunch, the school secretary is talking on the phone, or a student is crying in the background can be distracting and impersonal. I once made a phone call from the office to make an appointment and the person on the other end asked me if I was a war correspondent. "It sounds like people are running for their lives! Where are you?"

Notes Home

If your students' families have email, paper notes that come home with the student are usually reserved for communication from the office (unless those are emailed as well) and permission slips. If any families don't have email, be sure to include them in all communications by printing out a copy of the note and sending it home with the child. If it's a personal or important note for the family, put it in a sealed envelope and

> **BTW:** Simply because the majority of families use email doesn't mean you won't receive notes in your students' Homework Folders. Last-minute requests when parents don't have time to send you an email will arrive. Be sure to check the folders every day.

send it home. If you want an answer, place an extra piece of paper in the envelope with directions for a response: Are they to indicate when they can talk on the phone? Come in for a meeting? Be clear about the response you want to receive.

WHEN IS A PHONE CALL OR MEETING BEST?

If you're dealing with a sensitive subject, a phone call or meeting is more personal than an email. No one likes to receive an email containing bad news, especially about one's child. Consider how it would feel to read a message like this: "Sorry to tell you that your child got in a fistfight today. He will be spending the rest of the week in the office during lunch." Or this: "I just wanted to let you know that your child failed today's assessment and will most likely be repeating the grade."

A conversation is often needed to explain a situation, both what happened and what the plan is for moving ahead. If a child is in an altercation at school or the student is having an especially difficult day (meltdown, crying, totally bummed out), you want to be sure to tell the parents before the child does. Thoughtful communication with parents, especially about sensitive subjects, will gain their trust and cooperation. Be sensitive, put yourself in their shoes, and answer all their questions.

A MUTUALLY BENEFICIAL RELATIONSHIP

It's always beneficial to get to know the parents in your class. Help them be a part of their children's education by keeping them involved, up to date, and without any reasons to be unsatisfied with you. They'll be happier, and you'll have an easier time teaching their kids.

Chapter
SEVEN

Communicating with Families

Keeping parents involved in classroom life can be a struggle. Parents live busy lives and many have more than one child in school, sometimes in different locations. It can be hard for them to keep up. Consistent written communication about what's going on in the classroom can help keep them informed and encourage their participation in the education of their child. It can also help create a foundation for a healthy relationship between you, the student, and the parent. This chapter provides a summary of the types of written communication you'll be sending home and tips for doing each efficiently and effectively.

THE FIRST DAY OF SCHOOL NOTE HOME

The First Day of School Note Home is your chance to share who you are, deliver information about the coming year, and to request information from the parents. If it's thorough and well organized, it'll represent you well. This note sets the tone for the year.

Consider including the following topics in your note. They may not all apply to your situation, so use what does. If the note gets very long, you might want to spread it into two or three notes that you send home over the course of the first few weeks of school. Regardless, get the information home as quickly as possible so parents feel comfortable and you can begin collecting information about the families.

> **BTW:** If you teach in a neighborhood where English is not spoken by many of the parents, find someone who can help translate your note.

Information About You

Give families some biographical information about yourself, such as how long you've been teaching (and yes, be up front if it's your first year—everyone has one), where you went to school, where you received your training, where you're from, languages you speak, and any other information you would like to share. This isn't a résumé, so keep it short, no more than two paragraphs.

Attendance

Tell parents what time school starts and, depending upon the grade you teach, how documented tardiness affects the student's record. Include the process of what to do if students are late. (Do they go to the office, come straight to class, or go to another location in school?)

Communication

Let parents know how they can communicate with you, including your email address and the hours and days you check it (see pages 149–151), the school phone number, the Homework Folder, and any other way they can get in touch. Give the URL for your class website if you have one. Include your classroom visitation policy (see page 176). Let them know that if they don't have an email account, you'll check their child's Homework Folder every day. Don't let parents who don't have an email account feel like they are out of the loop.

Arrival and Dismissal

Include the time school starts and the time their child will be dismissed. Tell them where to pick up students after school and what happens if they're late (their child is sent to the office, will wait in your classroom, or whatever the system is at your school). Also include, if you know, where students will be brought if they attend after-school programs offered at your school.

Vital Information

Attach a Vital Information Sheet to the note. Offer to email it to families as well if they prefer to fill it out on their computer and email it back. (Your school may already have a version of this that they send out or that you can send out.)

The Vital Information Sheet should include the following:

- Name of child
- First and last names of parents
- All methods of communication for both parents, including phone numbers (home, cell, and work), email, and physical address (if they live in separate residences then both addresses)
- Who lives in the home (or homes) with the child to help with homework
- The languages spoken in the home
- The child's after-school schedule (parent pickup, after-school programs, classes, tutor, friend's house, grandma's house?), how they'll get there, and who will pick them up
- Known allergies (both to medicine and food) and health conditions you should know about

- Medications being taken
- Whether they will bring lunch or eat the school cafeteria lunch

Include a place on the Vital Information Sheet where families can indicate their interest in volunteering with the class. Ask:

- Can you make photocopies for the class?
- Do you want to volunteer on any field trips?
- Do you want to help in class or be a Class Parent?

It may seem like it's out of left field to ask parents to make copies for the class. Shouldn't that happen at school? In an ideal world, yes, it should. But depending upon where you teach, a broken copier can be as commonplace as a late student. I was teaching fifth grade and the copier had just broken. I needed about 150 copies of multiplication and division tests for the next few weeks. I looked back through the Vital Information Sheets and found a parent who said he could make copies. It got me out of a jam.

Finally, include a space on the Vital Information Sheet for parents to share any information they would like you to know about their child. What was their school experience like last year? What are their reading habits? What subjects do they like or find especially challenging? What would the parents like their child to accomplish this year? You'll glean a lot about your students from this information.

> **BTW:** Parents will often fill out forms such as the Vital Information Sheet and permission slips on their computer and email them to you saved as files that you cannot open and print. Tell them in advance which file types and versions you are able to use (Word, PDF, JPEG). I have received some attachments that I swear could only be opened by a computer programmer.

Be sure to add that you want to receive back the Vital Information Sheet no later than one week after school starts. This sheet will have the most up-to-date contact information available. Phone numbers, addresses, and email addresses can change over a summer, and the school may have contact information from kindergarten for students starting third grade!

Once you have all the Vital Information Sheets, you can use class rosters (see pages 44–46) to keep track of things like allergies and health issues, where kids go at dismissal, which parents want to volunteer, and so on. Find a way to conveniently track all the information you will commonly need, but keep the original Vital Information Sheets, too.

BTW: It's a great idea to find a parent to be a Class Parent. These super-volunteers can help in all sorts of ways, like organizing volunteers for fundraisers or special events, compiling the list of contact information into a class roster, or reaching out to difficult-to-contact parents. Sometimes other parents more readily respond to a fellow parent than they do to a teacher. Depending upon where you teach, it can be tough to get someone to be the Class Parent. In that case, splitting the role between a few parents might make it more likely that you'll get volunteers.

Local Walking Field Trip Permission Slip

If it's okay with your school, and if you teach somewhere that has places of interest within walking distance, include a Local Walking Permission Slip in your First Day of School Note Home. This permission slip will allow you to take students to the local park and other locations within walking distance of your school without having to send home a traditional permission slip every time. It can be a blanket permission slip that covers the entire school year. But check with your school first. A form may already be on file, or this kind of form may not be allowed.

In most school districts, a child is not legally allowed to go on a field trip without a signed permission slip. Don't take that rule lightly or you could find yourself in trouble.

Lunch and Snack

Let parents know when the kids will eat lunch in case they want to join in or help out at school. If a cafeteria menu is available, either in hard copy or online, tell parents how to get a hold of it.

If you want to have snack time in your class, explain how it will work in your classroom. Are students responsible for bringing their own or is it done as a group, with a rotating schedule? (A Class Parent can make this schedule for you.) Emphasize that snack foods need to be simple and easy to distribute. Avoid anything that needs to be refrigerated or that requires cutting or assembling. The snack, such as precut vegetables or fruit, should be ready to eat.

> I worked in a school where my class had lunch at 10:50 a.m. There was no point in giving them a snack in the morning, because by the time we got rolling it was time to pack up for lunch. The afternoons were long, and the kids were tired, so I gave them an afternoon snack plus a little healthy snack as they left school, just to make sure they had energy for wherever they were going.

It's exhausting to teach kids who are hyper on sugar. I only like to give out healthy snacks. Cookies, doughnuts, and the like are not distributed. A snack is meant to provide energy to work in school. Try to serve healthier snacks like fruit, low-sugar cereal bars, and crackers with cheese.

Homework

Explain your homework policy, the one you developed before the school year began (see page 72 in Chapter 3). Make a list of the items students will need for homework, such as a Homework Folder and a Homework Notebook, and how much work parents should expect their child to be doing per evening.

Physical Education

If there's a designated day (or days) of the week for P.E., tell parents what it is so they can be sure their child is dressed appropriately. Kids may need a water bottle, sneakers (no sandals or dressy shoes), a sun hat, sun protection, or warm clothes if you plan to be outside in cold weather.

Art

Art can get messy, which is usually a good thing—for the art. But when kids come to school in their finest and go home wearing a Jackson Pollack canvas, parents may not be too happy. Tell parents when the kids will have art or that you'll notify them when their child needs to bring a smock or art studio clothing. You can also have your students keep a smock at school.

BTW: Some parents will not be able to afford even the smallest admission fee for a field trip. Check with your school to see if it has any sort of financial aid available for field trips. If not, plan to have a few fundraisers early in the year to cover field trips so the fee doesn't come out of your pocket.

Field Trips

Be clear about the forms parents need to fill out so their child can attend scheduled field trips, and let them know there will often be a fee for those trips. Ask all parents to pay cash unless the trip is very expensive. I once got a check for 50 cents. If you do take a check for a trip, only accept checks made out to the school (verify this with the school administrator first). If a check bounces, the school will deal with it. Maybe the school has an online payment method as well. But for a smaller amount, I prefer to ask for cash.

I clearly state in the First Day of School Note Home that if I don't have a permission slip the day before the field trip, I will assume that the student is not joining us on that particular trip. Does this sound harsh? Yes. But parents need to hear the message that it's far more stressful for the teacher when parents wait until the last minute. If a child doesn't bring in the permission slip, obviously you cannot take him with you. He must spend the day with another class, which is no fun for anyone. (If a student brings the needed forms the day of the trip, I'll always take the child.)

Supplies

List the class supplies you need for the classroom (like glue, staples, copy paper, markers, tissues, and paper towels) and what the kids need for themselves (like journals and folders). If you teach in a neighborhood where families don't have the means to get supplies, check to see what resources the school has to offer before asking for anything from parents.

Include in this list a good backpack. I've seen kids come to school with their school supplies in a paper bag. It usually ends up with the lunches, covered in juice from an overripe piece of fruit, their supplies lost in a mess.

BTW: Backpacks can be expensive, so I always mention in my note that thrift stores are a handy resource for backpacks and lunch boxes, many of which are practically brand new.

Wish List

Some teachers post a wish list outside the classroom door of special items they want. This might include a small stereo to play music, a specific type of art supply, or something else that they will find useful to help their teaching. If you do this, keep it reasonable. This list is for items that go beyond regular school supplies—items that will make the classroom a nicer place or that will enhance the students' experience. Don't ask for a gift card to the local coffee house. If you're going to post a wish list, let the parents know in the First Day of School Note Home.

> **One teacher made a paper tree with paper apples hanging from branches. On each apple, she wrote one supply she needed for the classroom, such as glue, pencils, markers. Parents would take an apple or two, and she even added apples throughout the year when she felt something was needed in class.**

This first letter home is a lot of information for parents, but don't worry about that. As long as you keep it clearly organized and divided into topics (with headers), it provides what everyone needs to make it safely through the first few weeks of school without hassles. This First Day of School Note Home will be the first contact you make with many families. Make it count by keeping it simple and thorough.

If you teach in a neighborhood where English is not spoken by many of the parents, find someone who can help translate your note. All of this work will be for nothing if parents can't understand any of it.

BTW: Have a fellow teacher and/or someone in school leadership look over the note to make sure the systems you're using are in harmony with school policies.

THE WEEKLY NOTE HOME

Every Thursday afternoon or Friday morning I write a Weekly Note Home to the families. This keeps them updated about what's going on in class and any important upcoming events they should know about. I encourage them to ask questions if they have them. This note helps parents feel involved, aware, and comfortable with the school life of their child. I also post the Weekly Note Home on the door to the classroom so parents and other community members can read what we are up to when they are passing through the school.

Divide the note into topics, such as what is going to be covered in the next week broken up into subject areas like math, social studies, science, reading, writing, spelling, art, music, and physical education. Another topic might be upcoming special events such as field trips or class performances. If students will need special materials in the coming week or two, remind families in the Weekly Note Home. It doesn't need to be a catalog, just a simple letter filled with important information. You can also use the note home to highlight positive class achievements, like great performances, completed class art projects, or successful field trips. Make the letter easy to understand for all of your potential readers.

Encourage families to read the note together so everyone knows what's in store. Often, kids can answer their families' questions if you've been talking about upcoming subjects in class.

BTW: Some teachers like to send out a Monday Morning Note. I like sending the note on Friday so parents know what is coming up before the week starts and they can review it with their child over the weekend.

Of course, if something else comes up during the week, don't be shy about sending another note. Just because you write a weekly note doesn't mean that's the only time you're allowed to communicate with families.

PARENTS, THEIR CHILD, SOCIAL MEDIA, AND YOUR CLASSROOM

The presence of social media in the classroom is only increasing. Whether social media is your thing or not, every teacher needs to address it. The reason is simple. If your students are computer savvy (and who isn't these days?), it's likely many of them (particularly in upper elementary) will use some sort of social media network such as Facebook, Myspace, Twitter, YouTube, Flickr, Tumblr, Club Penguin, or one of the many others that are out there and that will continue to be developed as I write this book—even though many of them require users to be at least 13 years old. (Kids lie to get on, or their parents lie for them; it can be very hard to enforce such policies.) Interactions, both positive and negative, from the use of these networks will bleed into your classroom and there is little you can do to prevent it.

Your school may have a policy regarding social media; if so, let families know about it. But you probably can't do much to control interactions that occur outside of school. Parents may even tell you that it's none of your business what their child does on the computer at home or on their smartphone. Nonetheless, while it's not your role to monitor a child's goings-on after school, the ball is in your court once problems begin to play out at school.

Educating your students and their parents is the best way to manage possible problems. Most kids don't understand that when they write something online it is archived forever. "I deleted it," I've been told numerous times, "It's gone!" Wrong. Students need to be taught that anything said or done online stays online. (A lot of parents need to be taught this, too.) What they say can also be visible to many other people, other than the person or people with whom they're communicating.

> A student of mine, usually a beacon of positive energy, dragged her way to her desk one morning, slumped in her chair, and began to cry. She was the first student to arrive, so we had a few minutes to have a candid discussion. I asked her what was wrong and if she wanted to talk about it. Without raising her tear-stained face, she reached into her pocket and handed me a few crumpled-up pieces of paper. They were printouts of a conversation on a social media network among some fellow students in the class. Several classmates were calling her names that were pretty rough for anyone to digest, especially a 10-year-old. When the other students arrived, I sat with them and asked them what happened. They said they knew nothing and it was all lies. I pulled out the evidence. "But I erased that!" one exclaimed. I contacted the families in question immediately and told them they needed to monitor their children's use of the computer. It was affecting the learning environment, as well as the performance of others in class. Distressed, embarrassed, and angry, the parents apologized.

Let your students know that anything done online is permanent. Show them at school. Use a social media network in class and illustrate how, although they may erase something they wrote, it still possibly has been read by many others. It may remain in someone else's comment stream or elsewhere. Show them how anyone can take screen shots to save something you post. Using the interactive whiteboard so everyone can see, send

BTW: Cyberbullying laws are changing very quickly, as are school policies. Make sure you stay on top of what the laws are in your state or district as well as the policies at your school.

an email to yourself and then delete it. Then show them how easy it is to recover this email from the trash—for the sender *and* the recipient. I'll retrieve that same email from the trash a week later to reemphasize the point.

If you become aware of a problem with social media in your classroom, first, let someone else at school know, such as a fellow teacher, an assistant principal, a guidance counselor, the school psychologist, or even the principal. This is a good idea for three reasons. One, it establishes a record that you're working to take care of the issue. Two, you might get some good advice. If other teachers are dealing with similar issues, find out what they're doing or what you can do together. Three, these problems can escalate in a heartbeat and acting fast can help extinguish the issue quickly. That's why it's important to act quickly. Even if the student who is involved seems way too young to be saying such things online, intervene and get help fast.

As with most things regarding students' families, communication is key. Sending a note home to all the families in your class about the problem can help make families aware of a current problem as well as the potential hazards in general, even if some of them ignore it. Many parents sign up for the same social networks as their children so they can keep an eye on them. This is something that you can encourage. I don't recommend assuming a "watcher" role as a teacher. If you want to have a class Facebook page, you probably need to get this approved by your principal.

Even though we have to worry about the difficult effects of social media in school, don't let fear of problems stop you from using them in your teaching if that's your style. Many teachers use social media to connect with authors and kids in other parts of the world as well as to send out information like homework instructions for families and kids. The benefits of social media and the Internet in general far outweigh the potential problems.

Sample First Day of School Note Home

September 8

Dear Families,

Welcome! I hope you all had a wonderful summer and are ready for a great school year. I know I am! I look forward to working with you and helping your child grow to his or her fullest potential. I have an open-door policy, so if you have any questions, please stop by the classroom, send me an email at Otis45@xxx.com, or send a note in your child's Homework Folder. I will get back to you ASAP.

To tell you a little about me, this is my first year teaching. I received an MS.Ed in bilingual education at the Bank Street College of Education and did my student teaching at three different elementary schools, which included two first-grade classes and one fifth-grade class. Before teaching, I coordinated a homework help program for kids. I am really excited to begin my career with you and your children. I have been waiting for this for a long time.

This letter contains a lot of information you'll need to know in order to have a smooth school year, so please take the time to read it carefully, and again, please let me know if you have any questions. Thanks.

Communication

The best way to communicate with me is via email at Otis45@xxx.com. I check it often and will respond as soon as I can (though I may not check it over the weekend or in the evenings). Email is the easiest and most environmentally friendly way for me to keep in touch, and I will send home all notices, class notes, etc., via email **unless you request to receive hard copies.** Please let me know this week if you prefer hard copies.

To begin the year, please email me with your name, the name of your child, your phone number, and the email address you prefer to be contacted at so I can create a Class Contact List. This list will be distributed to all of the families in class, so please let me know if you prefer not to be on it. Thank you.

You can also reach me through the school phone: 555-555-1234.

Your student will receive a Homework Folder that goes home every night and comes back to school every morning. The Homework Folder will contain your student's homework for the evening, permission slips and other notes that need to be signed and returned, other school-wide notices, graded work, art work, etc.

(continued)

Please check the Homework Folder every evening, and if there are notes for you, take them out. Do not leave things in the Homework Folder. I will check students' Homework Folders every morning.

We have a class website that I will update regularly. It will have spelling lists, homework assignments, reminders, and much more information, so be sure to bookmark it and check it out often: www.ourschool.edu/5thgrade/kriegel

Arrival/Dismissal/Schedule/After School

School begins at 8:20 and dismissal is at 3:10. For the first few days of school, I will be meeting the children in the gym to take them up to class. After that initial period, students are to come up to class on their own.

My plan is for dismissal to be in the auditorium. Please pick up your child there—on time at 3:10—and leave the school promptly. Playing in the auditorium crowds the dismissal area and makes things more crazed than they need to be, so please don't allow your child to do it. To help ensure that every student goes to the right place, each student is required to shake my hand before leaving for his or her family, the bus, or the after-school program. If you arrive after 3:15, I will bring your child to the office.

Attendance

School begins at 8:20 a.m. Please make sure your child is here on time every day. If your student misses school, you can find missed assignments and homework on the class website or from another classmate. I am available by email, but generally everything you need to know will be on the website. If your child needs hard copies of homework missed, I will be sure to provide them.

Forms

Please fill out the attached Vital Information Sheet and return it. (I can also email you this form if you prefer to fill it out electronically and email it back to me; just let me know when you email your information for the Class Contact List.) Please sign the Local Walking Trip Permission Slip and return it to me as soon as possible.

On the back of the Vital Information Sheet (or via email), please include any information about your child that will help me get to know him or her better. What was last year's school experience like? What would you like to see him or her accomplish this year? How can I best support your child's growth?

(continued)

Snack/Lunch

Because the morning period is so long, we will break for a short mid-morning snack. I will send out a snack schedule that will show the days you are responsible for sending snack in for the class. I will only accept snacks such as fruits, precut vegetables, granola bars, crackers, pretzels, etc. (Cookies and other sweets will be sent home.) Please send snacks that are ready to serve so we don't have to spend class time preparing them. Thank you.

Our lunch period is from 12:30–1:20. After a 20-minute lunch period in the cafeteria students are sent to the playground for recess for 30 minutes.

Homework

Homework will be assigned each night unless otherwise noted. Subject matter will vary, but homework will always include a required minimum of 30 minutes of reading. Please keep up to date on what your child is reading. Your participation in his or her nightly reading is important. Homework will be checked every morning at the beginning of class and should be turned in via the Homework Folder. Besides the Homework Folder that travels back and forth between school and home with your child, all students need a small Homework Notebook in which they will write down the homework assignment each day.

Physical Education

I plan to do some sort of physical activity every day, in the classroom or outside. Please make sure your child wears appropriate clothing, including sneakers (or keeps a pair of sneakers in class labeled with his or her name).

Field Trips

I like to take a lot of field trips. For each field trip, unless we are touring the local neighborhood, I will need a signed permission slip from each child's family. I will send slips home two weeks or more in advance, and I appreciate it when families sign and return them quickly. It's stressful on the day of the trip when I'm still missing permission slips. If you do not turn in the permission slip by at least the day before the field trip I will assume your child is not joining us and will plan accordingly.

If a fee is associated with the field trip, please send that to me as soon as possible, too. I have financial aid available for field trips, so please let me know if you need it.   **(continued)**

Supplies

Here are the supplies your student will need. Please help your child get these this week.

- loose-leaf binder (Trapper Keeper)
- 1 package of loose-leaf paper (200 sheets)
- 10 loose-leaf dividers marked as follows: Writing, Science, Social Studies, Math, Spelling (we'll use the other 5 for other needs that come up)
- 1 small notebook to write down the homework assignment at the end of the day
- 2 two-pocket folders
- 1 small personal pencil sharpener with the student's name on it
- 2 composition books with at least 100 pages to be used for journals
- 1 graph paper notebook for math (not a pad, a notebook!)

The following supplies will be for the entire class to share. Please do not label with your child's name.

- 1 package of pencils (at least 10)
- 1 package of erasers (at least 5)
- 1 ream of white paper for drawing and/or the computer printer
- 1 box of tissues
- 1 roll of paper towels

Let me know if you have other things you would like to donate to the class, especially art supplies. I am sure I will have a use for them! Thanks.

When possible, "green" products (environmentally sensitive materials) are appreciated.

All students need a good backpack as well. You can usually find great backpacks in good shape at local thrift stores that are less expensive.

That's it for now. I look forward to meeting all of you soon and to having a great year.

Sincerely,
Otis Kriegel
Room 456
555-555-5678

Sample Weekly Note Home

March 17

Dear Families,

It has been great visiting with many of you during conferences. Thanks for coming in. It was a busy week here in Room 123, and next week will be the same.

Math

We have changed gears and are now working on fractions, percentages, and decimals. The math curriculum we use presents them all together, which makes it more natural for kids to understand. We are using many visual aids and manipulatives. Ask your student what we've been doing with Unifix Cubes!

Social Studies

Next Thursday we are heading to the Old Stone House in Brooklyn, the site of the Battle of Brooklyn, also known as the Battle of Long Island. We learned about the battle while watching *Liberty,* a documentary about the American Revolution. We will be taking more field trips to learn about the American Revolution in the next few weeks, including an upcoming trip to the Morris-Jumel Mansion in Washington Heights, where George Washington lived and from where he commanded the Continental Army. Please return your permission slips next week!

Writing

Next week we will begin working on sentence structure and parts of speech. Each student will be making a small flipbook with each page focusing on a part of speech. We will also be starting our next writing assignment, a persuasive letter based upon our study of the American Revolution.

Field Trips

Our upcoming trips are the following:

Thursday, March 24   Old Stone House, Brooklyn, NY (bring a bag lunch)

Tuesday, April 12   Morris-Jumel Mansion, NY, NY (bring a bag lunch)

Soccer

We are hoping to play outside again this week. It has been a lot of fun and the kids are getting in good shape!

As always, if you have any questions or concerns, please let me know. Have a terrific weekend!

Otis Kriegel

GETTING ON THE SAME PAGE

Written communication with your students' parents can form the backbone of your relationship with them, since they'll hear from you in writing far more often than they'll see you in person. It's important to be clear and direct, but also to have a little fun, if that's your style. Use this communication to show your personality and provide an easy and efficient way for families to participate in the school life of their children. All of these suggestions are meant to help you create a relationship with parents built on openness, honesty, and trust, which will help harmonize your efforts to help the child.

Chapter

EIGHT

When Families Come into the Classroom

Working face-to-face with parents can be stressful for even the most experienced classroom veteran. Still, if you have parents who are willing to meet you in person and work toward improving their child's classroom experience, take advantage of that opportunity to work as a team.

As with written communication, the goal of face-to-face communication is to involve parents in the classroom life of the child. But while personal contact with parents can enhance your ability to teach their child, it can also be a source of problems and thorny communication issues. It can take patience, much effort, and respect for personal and professional boundaries to make the relationship work for the three parties involved.

This chapter covers standard meetings such as Back to School Night as well as informal meetings. They're both ways you can make yourself accessible to parents and to make your relationships with them positive.

ENCOURAGING INVOLVEMENT

At some schools, the parents are eager and engaged, which is fantastic. At other schools, though, it's harder to get parents involved. Many of the ideas in this chapter are designed to encourage participation by parents, such as regularly communicating, having a clear classroom visitation policy, being empathetic to their individual situations, and being flexible to their individual needs. But two things can really help, especially with reluctant parent populations: attitude and opportunities.

Keep an open, positive attitude toward the families. Parents may be intimidated by schools, and if you welcome their questions and are flexible in terms of their schedules and when they can participate, this will encourage them to be more of a part of your classroom.

To create opportunities, think beyond parent-teacher conferences or Back to School Night. Consider sending out a weekly list with times when parents can sign up to help out in class or even just watch, or a list of activities or ongoing jobs they can do like participating in a poetry reading, a publishing party, a book club, or a class play. If parents' work has something to do with the curriculum, invite them to speak to the class or be interviewed by students for a writing assignment. There are multitudes of ways to encourage parents to be a part of the class. Make it easy for them, and many will do their best to come.

THE CLASSROOM DOOR: YOUR PARENT VISITATION POLICY

Many schools have policies in place that control the way parents can move around a school. Some schools are very strict about when parents can come in, others let them come and go as they please, and some require limited visiting times, usually near the beginning of the school day or by appointment only. It can be confusing to both parents and teachers. Sometimes learning the parent visitation policy is as difficult as understanding the fine print on your credit card statement. The important thing is, if your school has a visitation policy, you must learn it and abide by it. And communicate it to the families of your students.

If your school has a flexible policy, you most likely will receive a number of classroom visits, which may range from a parent standing at your door to one just barging right in. If that's the case, you'll want to set your own guidelines for when you want parents visiting your classroom. It's great to encourage parent involvement, but that doesn't mean letting parents march through your classroom at all hours of the day. Let them know your policy at the beginning of the year in your First Day of School Note Home (see page 156). Do what supports your teaching style and your students' learning.

I always prefer to have a liberal classroom visitation policy. Parents are invited to drop off their child at the door or watch the class—but that doesn't mean I make time to talk to them. If I'm teaching, that's my priority. They have to wait until I get a moment or I tell them to email me or stick a note to the classroom door and then I quickly return to teaching. You must be comfortable asserting your boundaries to employ this type of system.

When Is a Good Time to Visit?

A great time to have visitors is first thing in the morning, when your students are independently working. Be proud of your class! Let parents see your excellent management skills at work. This is not a time for a meeting with parents but an opportunity for them to spend a few passing moments watching your magic in action as the students start their day. It creates a community and makes parents feel a part of the classroom. And most times, kids love seeing their parents in school. Even if they feel embarrassed to give a kiss or hug good-bye, the kids feel loved and proud.

However, parents will (consciously and unconsciously) break your visitation guidelines. They need to be reminded. If a parent bursts into your room wanting to talk during the middle of the day, gently remind him or her to schedule a meeting time. There is no need to yell, scream, or call security.

On the other hand, if parents express an interest in participating in a classroom activity, I try to make room for them. I want to encourage this behavior, not dissuade it. This is especially important in communities where parent involvement is less frequent.

BTW: If an adult you don't recognize comes to your classroom, ask who he or she is looking for. You're responsible for knowing a lot of people, so don't feel bad if you don't recognize someone you've already met, especially at the beginning of the year. Keeping kids safe is more important than worrying about possible embarrassment. Also, some parents don't know where they are or where their kid is. I had a woman stride into my classroom berating me for letting her child go outside without a jacket. The child wasn't in my class, so I pointed her in the right direction. She didn't apologize but I'm sure she never made that mistake again—and she never came near my classroom again either.

Angry Parent Visits

As teachers, we don't know what stresses our students' parents. Be firm about your boundaries, but on the rare occasion when a parent comes into your room angry or combative during class, never engage in an argument or fight back in front of the class. You never want to pour gas on a fire, so doing your best to dissipate a potential conflict and discuss it at a later time is not only a wise move, but it models for your class how to keep your cool and effectively communicate under stress. It also shows your students, and the parent, that you're in complete control.

A parent pushed into a colleague's classroom, angry about an event that had happened the day before. Fuming, the woman began to raise her voice. In the middle of her tirade, she noticed that all of the students were silent and 28 sets of eyes were staring at her. The 29th set of eyes belonged to her daughter, who was completely humiliated.

> The teacher, the essence of calm during any emotional storm, quietly walked the mother to the door, comforting her by acknowledging her anger and gently, but firmly, saying this was not the time to talk but she would be sure to make time for a discussion. The woman, feeling foolish and uncomfortable after seeing the response of the class and her daughter, agreed to return later.

In general, try to give parents the benefit of the doubt. Usually they're doing the best they can. Empathy goes a long way. But you'll often have parents who will continue to break your clearly stated rules, and they, just like your students, need to be reminded of them. Be firm and you'll win their respect (most of the time), and they'll likely remember to follow your guidelines in the future.

At the same time, if you feel threatened or believe that you might be in danger due to a parent's behavior, call security immediately. You can also call (or yell, if need be) for a neighboring teacher. The majority of upset parents will calm down when you listen to them and you show that you genuinely care about what they're saying. But in the uncommon, unfortunate situation when a parent, whose fists are clenched and voice seems to be getting louder and louder, will show no signs of wanting to communicate in a peaceful way, get help fast from a fellow teacher and your administration immediately. Don't wait. Talk to your principal about any parent who is a chronic problem.

THE SMOOTH MEET THE TEACHER NIGHT

Whether it's called "Meet the Teacher," "Back to School," or "Parents' Night," many teachers—especially the ones new to the profession or new to the school—get the jitters before they have to stand up and speak to a group of their students' parents. Your mind may be a jumble of what-ifs: "What if they ask me a question I can't answer? What if I give out the wrong information? What if I forget to tell them something? What if I do something awful, like sweat through my shirt or pass out? Or what if nobody shows up?"

It can be scary, but this evening can actually be a lot of fun.

It may help calm your nerves to remember that parents are here because they care. While it's possible that a parent or two may come with a chip on their shoulder, most parents want information and reassurance. This night is for them to get to meet you, the person who is spending the majority of the year with their children. It's understandable that they have a vested interest in you. That's a good thing.

Many new teachers, if they don't have children of their own, don't know what parents are looking for this night. Take a moment and think about what you would want to know about your child's teacher. Do you think you'd want to know her credentials? Would you want to see a person who is competent, can communicate, and loves what she does? To prepare yourself and put to rest some of the butterflies in your stomach, write down a few questions that you'd want to ask about your child's teacher and answer them.

BTW: One teacher told me about his Meet the Teacher Night: "I want parents to see that I have good energy, am a thoughtful person, and know what I'm doing. Period. That takes no longer than 30 to 45 minutes." Many parents will arrive to Meet the Teacher Night after having been at work all day. They're likely to be tired, so a drawn-out, boring presentation isn't going to win you any awards. They want to see that you're a positive, caring person with good intentions, who can communicate and is going to work hard to educate their kid.

Preparing for the Evening

You don't need to hire an event planner to make this evening successful. With a few simple steps and a little thinking ahead, you should be fine. By the end of the meeting, parents should feel more involved in their child's classroom, have an understanding of what is to be taught and when, and be comfortable with you as their child's teacher.

In one school where I taught, teachers provided beverages and snacks and were dressed for entertaining. I thought a pair of pressed, clean pants and a collared shirt was enough. It seemed absurd to do more. Parents were coming to learn about their child's teacher, not for a tea party. I didn't offer food and/or drinks (and never have), and I was leaving the school after what I felt was a successful, 40-minute meeting, as other teachers were cursing as they cleaned up their rooms late into the evening. You want to show parents you appreciate that they've taken time out of their busy lives to attend, so a snack can be a nice touch, but it's not mandatory. A well-organized, informative meeting is something most parents will really appreciate. On the other hand, you may want to find out the expectations of your principal. If he wants you to do something fancy, you'll probably want to do it.

Sign-in sheet. Create a sign-in sheet so parents can write down their name and the name of the child they belong to. If any families haven't turned in their Vital Information Sheet, plan to have it available so they can fill it out immediately.

Information sheet. Make an information sheet with the dates of state tests, parent-teacher conferences, and major field trips or events. Also include the basic weekly schedule, including any special classes like art, gym, or music. Even though you'll talk about these details during the meeting, they can read this while they wait and take a hard copy with them to keep at home. See page 183 for a sample Meet the Teacher Night Information Sheet.

Volunteer sheets. Prepare sign-up sheets for any field trips you have planned or any classroom volunteer roles you know you'll want to have filled.

BTW: Depending upon your class, you may need a translator to communicate with a large percentage of the parents. Be sure to prepare the written material for this as well. When I taught in a bilingual classroom, I would either provide a simultaneous translation or hold two separate meetings.

Sample Meet the Teacher Night Information Sheet

Meet the Teacher Night
Otis Kriegel, 5th Grade

Test Dates
English Language Arts (ELA): May 4–6
Math: May 11–13

Other Important Dates
Parent-teacher conferences:
 Tuesday, Nov. 9 afternoon
 Wednesday, Nov. 10, evening
 Tuesday, March 15, afternoon
 Wednesday, March 16, evening

Overnight field trip:
 Wednesday–Friday, Feb. 9–11

Outside-the-Classroom Schedule
Monday: Art 10:45
Tuesday: Games 9:05, Library 1:25
Wednesday: Soccer 9:30 (wear sneakers!)
Thursday: Dance 10:45
Friday: Computers 9:05, Music 9:55

Short assignment. Next, plan for parents to have something to do at the beginning of the meeting while everyone is settling in. This helps set a fun tone. For the lower grades, ask them to write their child a note and put it in the blue homework basket in the front of the classroom. In the upper grades, give parents a geography test, a math problem, or even a spelling test they can complete independently. Write your instructions on the board and watch who follows directions. Some will ignore the work while others will work in teams and laugh their way through it. You may figure out which parents belong to which children in a matter of minutes.

BTW: Depending upon the community in which you teach, some parents may have received little education themselves. Be conscious of this as you create a short, fun assignment for them to complete while they wait for you to start the meeting. Don't make them feel insecure or bad. The objective is to encourage parent involvement, not scare people away.

Tomorrow's schedule. Write up the following day's schedule on the board, just as you would any other day. Parents love to see this "real-life" example.

Tonight's agenda. Finally, create an agenda for the evening and write it on the board. This not only cues parents to what you're going to cover during the meeting, it will also help you remember what information you want to share. If you're nervous—and you probably will be—this will help you out a lot.

Getting Through the Evening

The following list is an example of agenda topics that you can use for your meeting. Add and subtract to this list to make it work for you and your classroom, school, and community of families.

BTW: Before you start the meeting, remember that parents are going to have a lot of questions. Ask them to hold questions until the end so you can get through the information. In the meantime, their questions might be answered.

Welcome. Talk about yourself, where you're from, why you wanted to teach, pertinent interests, and any other details you'd like to add. Keep it to less than two minutes. Then have parents introduce themselves to the group and say which child they belong to, especially if you haven't met the majority of the parents. Besides being helpful to you, it's nice for parents to see who is who, especially if their kids have been talking about new friends in class. Point out the agenda on the board before you begin working your way through it.

Daily schedule. Refer to the information sheet you created and review the daily schedule, noting any special classes the kids go to during the week such as art, dance, library, media, or music. Point out tomorrow's schedule on the board.

Main subjects. Give parents a general idea of what the kids will be learning this year. Make it a broad overview. There's no need to go through the details like, "In January we will be studying decimals. In February we will be doing decimal division."

> I was at the home of friends one evening for dinner and they were talking about their child's teacher. They loved her. She was smart, funny, and dedicated, and their daughter really enjoyed the class. The year was going well and almost over (it was May), but the teacher had promised at Meet the Teacher Night that they were going to do a class play in the beginning of spring as part of the science curriculum, and it never happened. The kids were bummed, and so were the parents, but the teacher never addressed it again. I explained to them that it had happened to me; I had overpromised and not been able to deliver. They said, "But she didn't apologize or explain it to the kids at all." That's why it's usually a good idea to keep your discussion of the subjects general at Meet the Teacher Night. If you promise something, make sure you can deliver. If you later find you can't, step up and apologize.

Field trips. Explain the use of permission slips, fees, and what parents should do if they want to volunteer. Let them know that you need permission slips and fees well before the day of the trip and that fees should be paid in cash, unless it's for a more expensive field trip (see page 162). Encourage them to volunteer, but let them know that parent volunteers are not there for "the ride" or to spend quality time with their child. They're there to help the teacher and support the entire class. They should come because they want to help (see page 200).

Homework policy. Describe your homework policy (page 72) and show parents your Homework Record Book so they know you mean business.

Classroom visit policy. Explain your policy clearly. This should be a review of what you shared in the First Day of School Note Home. See page 176.

Standardized tests. For better or worse, testing is on everyone's mind these days. Keep this discussion to the basics. Discuss when the tests are (and point it out on the sheet you handed out earlier in the evening), what you do to prepare your students, and what parents can do to help (which is mostly to stay calm and make sure the student gets a good night's sleep the night before).

Report cards. Tell parents when they'll receive a copy and how (email, mail, or sent home with the student). If you send home copies, tell them that they'll receive the original at the end of the year if that is true.

Parent-teacher conferences. Point out on the information sheet when conferences will take place, the expected length of these meetings, and how they can sign up (see page 191). If your parent-teacher conferences are coming up relatively soon, it's a great idea to have parents sign up now, while you have them in the room. If it's too far in the future (more than a month), save it for later.

How to get in touch. List the methods they can use to contact you. See page 149.

Volunteering in class. Besides field trips, which you've already discussed, parents can volunteer in class or organize fundraisers or class events (like a class party). Refer them to the volunteering sign-up sheets and encourage them to sign up for something before they leave at the end of the meeting.

Middle school. If you teach in a K–5 school and there are choices for middle schools, then the fifth-grade meeting must address the process. Find out the information you need before the meeting.

Questions. This is the time when you'll field questions about everything from testing to cafeteria food to curriculum. Do your best to answer everyone's questions, but remember, this evening isn't about individual kids; it's about the class as a whole. You may also have parents asking specific questions about policies, curriculum, or plans far into the future. If you don't know the answer to a parent's question, don't make something up. Write down the question and tell the parent you'll find out the answer and get back to him or her. Then don't forget to do it!

> At the end of one Meet the Teacher Night, a parent approached me and asked, "So tell me, how is my child doing and what are your plans to improve her reading?" I said, "I don't discuss individual students on Meet the Teacher Night. Otherwise, I'd never get through all of the information I presented. Let's talk at parent-teacher conferences. If you have a concern, please email me and we can discuss it sooner, but not tonight."

BTW: Kindergarten is usually the most intense Meet the Teacher Night, because parents can be relatively new to parenting and especially to having a child in school. If you're teaching kindergarten, set aside more time to answer questions at the end, because parents will have a million!

SHARING BAD NEWS

My rule is simple and to the point:

Never share bad news alone.

Bad news includes any information that is not complimentary or could be potentially difficult for parents to hear, such as a child failing the grade, being referred for testing for a potential learning challenge, displaying continued poor behavior, or being involved in a bullying incident. When we hear information that is uncomfortable or hard to digest, we can react in unpredictable ways. Yelling, getting defensive, crying, or blaming someone or something else are all possible responses. If you need to share any news of this type with a parent, be sure that someone else is present during the meeting. This person can be the principal (rarely), the assistant principal, a guidance counselor, the school psychologist, or even a fellow teacher. For the most part, these conversations will go relatively smoothly, but in the case that one doesn't, you need someone not only to support you, but also to act as a witness to the conversation in case it's referred to during a later meeting. In the worst possible case—if emotions escalate—the witness can call for an administrator (if he or she isn't one).

BTW: Whatever the bad news, always have evidence, documentation, or extra information to support whatever you're stating. This will help the parents understand and you'll appear more competent and committed to helping the child.

If you're making a phone call, ask someone to sit with you and listen to what you're saying to make sure you stay calm and collected and to be witness to your side of the conversation.

When you're talking with the parent about bad news, be sensitive. Even if the parent is emotional or irrational, remember that you're not giving bad news about a computer that cannot be repaired; it's about the parent's child, one of the most important parts of his or her life. Make the meeting the beginning of a conversation about how you and the parents can help remedy the situation. That might mean extra help for a struggling student, a change in seat assignments, or other interventions to help the child. This keeps the tone positive and puts the focus on improving in the future instead of dwelling on the past. Most parents will appreciate that you're taking the time to communicate with them openly about their child, even if it's something that is not flattering or is hard to accept.

GETTING YOURSELF THROUGH THE PILE: REPORT CARDS

I don't know anyone who looks forward to writing report cards. It's like trying to communicate what could be an hour-long conversation on a 3" x 5" index card.

Whether your school or district requires you to write in-depth narrative explanations of the child, fill in numbers, make checks in boxes, or do a mix of all three, it's a challenge to communicate a student's progress, personality, and other qualities in this report. With any luck, the parents will sign up for a parent-teacher conference, so you'll get the opportunity to further explain yourself then.

If you're required to write narratives, talk to another teacher about some of the key phrases that are used to describe a child and what is expected at your school. Some schools hand out a list of euphemisms to use when writing reports and/or speaking to parents. They can be pretty funny. For example: "Sarah has been trying to play more fairly with others" may actually mean "Sarah has only been in a few fights this year." "Miguel's cursive is improving" means "I'm able to read what Miguel writes." Several books and websites are filled with euphemisms that teachers use to smooth out the truth a bit. Although you must be clear, sometimes using one or two can at least get the conversation started in a way that will be easier for the parent to digest.

For example, here are two different ways to say Morgana is struggling with reading:

- "Morgana is not doing well in reading."
- "Morgana is reading slightly below grade level, but she is working hard."

Whether the child is excelling or finding school difficult, you want to use expressions that are both efficient and sensitive to the parent and to the child. If you want the parents to participate in their child's education and your classroom, the report card should teach them about their child as a student and explain how they can help. Don't alienate them with hard-edged feedback or educational jargon that parents might not understand and may even resent.

BTW: Remember, if your students can read, they're likely to read the reports, too. I like to write reports so everyone in the family can understand them and the kid can agree, disagree, or discuss the report with you and her family.

The more specific the report is, the better. Explain what a child needs to do to improve in a certain area. For example, if Luther is having a hard time with his basic addition skills, provide some ideas of what he and his parents can do to help: "Because Luther is having a hard time with his basic addition skills, it would help him to review the addition combinations that add up to 10 (3+7, 6+4, etc.)." This starts the parents off in the right direction; it lets them know the problem and what they can do to help remedy it. Otherwise, you leave the parent hanging helplessly with bad news and nowhere to go. It's like being in a dark room with no light switch.

After you write a number of report cards, don't be afraid to copy and paste phrases or sentences that can be used again. Every report card is unique to that student, but that doesn't mean you can't use some of the wording you developed for another kid's report. Recycle those brilliant phrases you make up.

Last but not least, know your audience. Who are the parents? What are they like? Do they like to hear information in a more blunt fashion or are they very sensitive? Do they have a strong command of the English language or would it be best for you to have the report translated? Think about who they are and how best to communicate with them. Will they feel cheated if you don't write a lot or be exhausted by having to read so much?

> **BTW:** If report cards aren't stored electronically, make copies and only give out the original at the end of the year. Hold onto a copy for either one year (another teacher or specialist might want to refer to it) or until the student has graduated from the school. A third option is to put a copy in the student's permanent record or in a portfolio. Your school may have a policy for how to handle storage of report cards.

PARENT-TEACHER CONFERENCES

Maybe you imagine a parent who arrives on time, reads the report card, shakes your hand, and says, "Thanks so much" without even asking a question. Or maybe you imagine being cornered by two angry parents, or having such great conversations that you run way over the allotted time, making everyone waiting late. Some of these scenarios and many others are likely to happen, so it's best to prepare yourself as much as you can.

Meeting with parents and/or families individually can be an incredibly useful time for all involved. It gives you a chance to discuss the student in depth and share information, involving the parent in an aspect of the child's life he or she might not know much about. It's an enormous time commitment, but one that is worthwhile for all parties involved. So how do you make it a successful meeting? And how do you schedule all of these meetings?

Making a Schedule That Works

Scheduling is almost as important as the meeting itself. To make a schedule, you must know how long your conferences will be. If your school has a prescribed amount, follow the lead your first year. If you get to decide, I suggest a 20-minute conference. That gives just enough time to talk casually with no one feeling rushed. It's a big time commitment when you add up 20 minutes for all your kids, but it's very worthwhile, especially for the first conference of the year.

Many schools and teachers like a 10-minute conference, but I think that's too short. You just get started when you hear a knock on the door. Ending a meeting prematurely and needing to schedule another one because the conversation was cut off is inefficient and defeats the purpose. Schedule enough time so you don't need to arrange another meeting the following week.

Create a schedule of 20-minute blocks with a five-minute break in-between every third or fourth conference. That gives you just enough time for a restroom break and maybe to have a snack, make a phone call, or take a quick walk down the hallway to breathe.

Send the schedule home to families and ask each family to request their top three choices of times for their conference labeled 1, 2, and 3, and send it back by email or with the student in the Homework Folder. Then go through the requests and arrange the schedule so it works for everyone. If you know the families can make it to school, hang a sign-up sheet outside your door or in the lobby and let them sign up on a first come, first served basis. You can also use Google Docs or something similar to host a sign-up sheet on your class website if your families have Internet access.

Whatever method you use for sign-ups, check to make sure you've heard from everyone. If a family hasn't signed up, make a phone call to find out why. Encourage them to sign up, or work to find a time that works for them. This may be all you need to do to get them to participate more.

> **BTW:** If parents arrive early, have examples of work in the hallway for them to look at. For the lower grades, provide favorite books being read aloud in class as well.

Wait until you get the majority of the sign-up sheets back before you send out the schedule, but try to do it at least two weeks before the meetings so everyone has plenty of time to accommodate their schedules and coordinate with other family members, partners, and spouses. Receiving the conference schedule will serve as a good reminder for the families who have yet to sign up. If you have families signing up late, continue to fill up the schedule even after the week of conferences has begun.

> A friend with whom I taught didn't believe in only having conferences during the allotted period, which was one afternoon and one evening. "How can parents all come at those times? It isn't fair and I want to meet with families," he told me. He spread out his conferences over a 10-day period. The percentage of parents with whom he was able to meet jumped significantly. All he did was add a time slot in the morning, before school, and one or two in the afternoons. I adopted the same attitude and idea, and have found that I usually meet with the majority of families. It's worth the extra time.

Sample Parent-Teacher Conferences Schedule

It's time for the Fall Parent-Teacher Conferences. Please sign up for three different times, marking your order of preference (1st, 2nd, 3rd), and I will do my best to accommodate all of you. Please email your preferences or return this form in your child's Homework Folder by Monday, October 23. I will send out the final schedule at least a week before the conferences begin.

Thank you and I look forward to seeing all of you.

Tuesday 11/09	Wednesday 11/10	Friday 11/12
7:50 am _____	7:50 am _____	7:50 am _____
12:30 pm _____	3:35 pm _____	3:30 pm _____
12:50 pm _____	3:55 pm _____	**Wednesday 11/17**
1:10 pm _____	4:15 pm _____	8:00 am _____
1:30 pm _____	4:40 pm _____	3:30 pm _____
1:55 pm _____	5:00 pm _____	**Thursday 11/18**
2:15 pm _____	5:20 pm _____	8:00 am _____
2:35 pm _____	5:40 pm _____	3:30 pm _____
2:55 pm _____	6:05 pm _____	**Friday 11/19**
3:20 pm _____	6:25 pm _____	8:00 am _____
3:40 pm _____	6:45 pm _____	3:30 pm _____
4:00 pm _____	7:05 pm _____	3:50 pm _____

To help me stay on time, please arrive on time for your scheduled slot. If you are late, that time will come out of your scheduled meeting. If you cannot make your scheduled time, please let me know in advance and I will be happy to reschedule a time that works for you.

A few quick tips about scheduling the fun and more difficult conferences:

- Try not to schedule what you expect to be more challenging conferences all in a row. Spread them out over the week. That'll help keep you from burning out.

- Schedule those difficult conferences that you think might run overtime in the morning. The arrival of your students at your classroom door is a natural ending to the meeting. You can also arrange potentially difficult meetings so you have another conference immediately afterward.

- Always try to end your evening conference schedule on a good note, with parents you think will be fun to speak with.

Who Should Come to the Conference?

Let's hope someone shows up! Sometimes parents attend together and sometimes one parent comes alone. Sometimes you'll get another family member, such as a grandparent, an aunt, an uncle, a cousin, or a brother. I have also had an entire extended family show up in addition to the parents. Ten people were in my classroom and everyone was excited to be there. That was fun!

I always encourage students to attend a conference. They can learn to speak for themselves and talk about aspects where they feel successful, challenged, or confused in class. Parents get to hear their child talk about school, which for some will be a rarity.

The only time when including a student in the conference is not recommended is if you need to discuss a topic in private, such as a potential learning challenge or a series of severe events in class. In this case, tell the parents you'd like to meet with them without the student, or only include the student for the first few minutes of the conference. And remember, if you think the parents will have a hard time digesting that information: "Never give bad news alone." Bring a colleague with you to the conference.

Share the Report Card Before the Meeting

To prepare everyone for the conference, do your best to get the report card to the families beforehand. That way, no one gets any surprises, and parents can begin to formulate questions before the meeting. If the conference is the first time they've seen the report, and some grades are lower than anticipated, half the meeting will be spent explaining the reasons and what the student can do to improve in these areas.

What Do I Say During the Conference?

So what do you do in the meeting? What is there to say? Can you anticipate what questions parents are going to ask? What if they won't leave on time?

You can't predict every moment of parent-teacher meetings. But you can do a number of things to prepare, the most important being to plan for a conversation, not a business meeting. You're talking about their child, not a product or sales report. Make it as comfortable as possible for everyone by addressing matters with sensitivity.

There are many ways to lead a parent-teacher conference. Here is one method. It won't take you long to establish your own meeting structure.

Start positive. First, before addressing the report card, quickly mention a few positive points about the child. What is she doing well? Tell a funny or heartwarming story about her in class, something that will make the family feel good about the kid, even if she hasn't had many bright spots. (Think about what you'll say about each student ahead of time, so you're not scrambling to think of something in the moment.) This relaxes everyone, even if they know some bad news is right around the corner.

Use the report card to get the conversation going. Next, review the report card. If this is the first time parents have seen it, give them some time to look it over. If they brought their copy and already went over it, simply ask them if they have any questions. One of my favorite questions to use as a lead into discussing the report card is, "Does this report look like your child? Does it seem accurate?"

BTW: If parents have complaints or problems, listen to them thoughtfully. Restate what you hear them say to be sure you heard their concerns correctly, which acknowledges the parents' worry or dispute and lets them know they're being heard. Use this as a starting point to offer insights and solutions. For example, "I hear that you're concerned about your daughter's understanding of bar graphs, so I have arranged for her to work with me twice a week in a small group as well as once a week during lunch." Work with the parents; don't fight them. If you feel yourself getting defensive, take a breath and try again.

I once had a conference about a student who was new to the school and doing great. I was excited to share the good news, but figured the parents already knew. The kid was an angel in class. She was hardworking, always helped others, participated, had a great sense of humor, and was a true pleasure to everyone around her. The student's mom came in, looking exhausted. She smacked the table with the weight of a boxer's punch, the report card now under the weight of her hand. Then she began to cry and said, "You cannot imagine how happy I am. She is just a demon at home! This report doesn't seem anything like her! What am I doing wrong?" I was sorry to hear of the mom's struggles with her daughter at home, but I learned something important: kids behave differently in different environments. (It may sound obvious now, but it's important to remind yourself of this truth.) The conference was a time for both of us to share what was and what wasn't working at home and at school. We learned from each other.

Areas of excellence and room for improvement. After discussing the report card, address some specific positives about the child related to the report card (more specific than the casual positive points you began the conference with). Use the report card as a map, pointing to areas of success. Then, lead this into the areas of needed growth, where the student is either struggling or isn't working up to his potential.

Stay away from phrases that are too aggressive, such as "not getting it," "really far behind," and "doesn't understand," which can feel to the parent like a final judgment. Find gentler but truthful ways to communicate some of the challenges. Phrases like "struggling," "this is a challenge for him," and "we're still working on this" can make some tough news easier to digest and can open up discussion about ways to help the child. Don't avoid the truth, but package it in a way that shows parents that by working with you, they can help their child improve. Think of it as preparing vegetables for a kid who hates them; putting a plate of raw carrots and broccoli in front of him isn't going to get him to eat it, but cooking the vegetables with a little olive oil will make them a lot more appetizing.

Don't just tell, show: Use work samples. Now you'll know why you're keeping such a thorough student portfolio or file of student work for each kid (page 71). Use those examples to make points about the student's performance. Many parents will be open to hearing constructive feedback about their child, but some will refuse to believe that their child can struggle with anything. In those cases, use the student's work to prove your point, and, most importantly, clearly explain your expectations. What does the student need to do to improve? What are you going to do to help make this happen, and what can the family do as well? How are these changes going to benefit the student? Promise to share any changes, both positive and negative, that you observe as the year goes on.

Expectations for the future. To finish, review your expectations for the student during the next semester. What will he be expected to work on? How can he continue to improve, and what are you planning to do to make that happen? What can the parent do to help?

Parents will also want to ask questions. Unlike at Meet the Teacher Night, I always encourage questions throughout the conference, not just at the end. Listen to parents, answer their questions, and use their inquiries as a means to lead you to other topics of discussion. The more you explain to parents, the more they'll feel involved and heard, which will increase their trust in you and the school—and the more they'll share, as well. That helps you learn as much as you can from them.

BTW: Keep to your schedule. If a parent is late, that time comes out of that parent's conference. It may sound harsh, but otherwise you'll be running an hour late before you know it, and that's not only a pain for you, it's unfair to other parents who show up on time and end up waiting in the hallway, sitting in chairs that are two sizes too small for them. I recommend you arrange the seating during conferences so you face a clock in your classroom. That way you can keep an eye on the time without checking your watch every five minutes.

YOUR VOLUNTEER SQUAD

Parents can be an enormous help. From field trips to in-class projects, they can provide you with the support you need to be more successful in the classroom. Many parents really love it, too, though some of them feel intimidated or don't have time to volunteer, even though they would like to. If you create opportunities at many different times and lengths, you make volunteering more appealing and accessible, giving more parents the chance to be involved. Fifteen minutes of in-class, one-on-one help with a student during a work time is better than nothing at all. I'll take that any day of the week.

The majority of parents who volunteer in class or on field trips will be cheerful and helpful. They want to help out and be a part of the classroom world you have created. It's an exciting opportunity for them, and most are as thrilled as kids on the first day of school. They ask what they can do to help, and although they'll spend some time with their child, they know they are there to help the entire class. With clear instructions about your expectations, you can assign some of them rather difficult chores, such as being the partner of a more challenging child, managing a reading group, conducting an art project or science experiment, or communicating with tour guides on a field trip.

Parent volunteers are also great because you can learn from them by watching the way they communicate or work with kids in the class, many of whom they may know outside of school (not only their own kids, but their neighbors and their kids' friends). You can learn what these students like or dislike, or new ways to connect with them.

I've also had the unfortunate experience of parent volunteers who do anything but help. Sometimes you have to take what you can get, but if you're lucky enough to have a number of parents who want to volunteer, it's up to you to decide who will do what. Try to get the more reliable parents in roles that require them to be reliable, and try to put less helpful parents in less complicated roles, like simply walking with kids or carrying lunches—both of which are important as well.

> **It was going to be a long day. We were heading to the museum and I knew my first-grade class was going to be tired by midmorning. I brought a snack for them to eat before we entered the museum to make sure there were no meltdowns when I wanted their brains functioning. I sat them down outside of the museum and asked one of the parents who joined us to bring the snack I had asked her to carry. She looked at me, crumbs covering her chin, and shrugged. "I thought some was for me for coming on the trip and the rest I left at school." Another lesson learned: Give clear instructions about everything—even the snack!**

So how do you know what to assign to whom? Try to get to know families before you need volunteers. If you've had your Meet the Teacher Night and met some parents during conferences, that's a good start. You can also take a few local trips that last no more than a couple of hours, and invite parents to come so you can check them out and see how they work with the class. If you don't have the opportunity to test-run a parent, do your best to judge who will really be of help to you and the class.

If you're uncomfortable around certain parents, set up times for them to volunteer when you feel at ease, whether that means doing an in-class project, going on a shorter field trip, or just walking to the park. Their presence is meant to support you and your teaching, not give you more to manage. If it's too late, and they've already volunteered for a longer field trip or more intensive in-class project, be sure you have other volunteers who you can trust to help out.

Volunteering in Class

Having parents volunteer in the classroom is a great way to include them in the students' work as well as get some valuable extra help. You can have them help manage art projects or science projects, work with students in one-on-one reading time, run book clubs or small groups, read to the class, sort Homework Folders, prepare supplies or handouts for activities, and a lot more.

You can have parents come in for a certain time of day, to do a certain project, or all day. Whatever you decide, think through exactly what you want them to do before they arrive so you have specific assignments for them. If you don't, don't expect too much from them.

After a particularly good experience, parents will speak with others and share the positive news, which will encourage more participation. They'll also feel more a part of their child's education, which can be a missing link for certain kids. Offer ample opportunities for parents to help out in class to increase their participation and encourage them to be a part of the community.

Volunteering on a Field Trip

Most parents who join you on a field trip will be very helpful, watching the kids, taking responsibility of a small group of students, making sure everyone eats lunch and cleans up after themselves (no one likes a class that litters), and being respectful in public. But you may also have less helpful parents, like that parent who's going to chain smoke, talk on her cell phone, or smother her child with attention the entire time.

Don't blame that parent too quickly. She most likely wants to help and is doing her best, but she's just not sure what she can do to help you out. It's your job to manage the trip, including students and volunteers. Part of that means teaching volunteers how to be better helpers by assigning tasks that will keep them both busy and useful. Make a list of jobs to occupy them on the field trip. For instance:

- Take roll of the class every half hour, counting heads to make sure everyone is there (although you should do that several times, too)

- Alphabetize the permission slips

- Before the trip, pick up extra lunches from the cafeteria for students who forgot their own

- Be a class crossing guard, always slightly ahead of the class

> **BTW:** Make the stellar parent volunteer a role model by having him or her help you train the others.

> Each week I took my class to play soccer, and one parent always wanted to join us. The first week he did nothing and even stepped into the game occasionally to help out his own kid, upsetting the other students in the process. He ignored my requests to help everyone, and finally I realized that he didn't want to listen to me and wasn't going to change. Another parent, who volunteered weekly, was terrific. I asked him if I could pair him with the other parent. He didn't mind at all, and because the other parent was more willing to listen to him, he was able to get him to be a little more helpful.

BEFRIENDING A PARENT: A GOOD OR BAD IDEA?

Some parents will feel like friends from the moment you meet them. You'll feel comfortable talking, even socializing, with them. Many teachers cultivate friendships with parents. Over the years, I have met some of my closest friends through being their child's teacher. But I usually waited until their child wasn't in my class any longer or until close to the end of the year to initiate a friendship. That includes "friending" parents or connecting with them on social media: I recommend waiting until their child is no longer your student.

> A teacher I knew became fast friends with a parent at the beginning of the year and they regularly socialized on Friday afternoons. The teacher was in her third year and felt comfortable and confident that she had the job under control. But then her friend's child started struggling, and she began to spend a lot of extra time with the student. Soon, a few other students complained. "You're always helping him because you're friends with his mom," one said. She hadn't even realized it. When she backed off a bit, the mother complained. Now she was in the middle of professional responsibilities and a friendship, and things got messy.

Yes, some teachers meet their future spouses at parent-teacher conferences, and close friendships have been born from the classroom connection. Just be aware. You're a powerful member of the community. You need to do your job with as little bias as possible. Don't isolate yourself, but be aware, and be fair.

BTW: If you do befriend a parent, or are already friends with a parent of a student, never talk about other students or work issues with them. These are meant to be confidential. You'd be surprised how rumors and gossip can fly through the hallways of a school.

WORKING WITH PARENTS IS A BIG PART OF THE JOB

Parents can play a key role in the education of your students and in your success as a teacher. You can cultivate connections with parents in many ways, but mainly through clear, open, honest, regular communication. Do your best to become as comfortable as you can when working with parents and to create many easy opportunities for them to be involved in their child's school life. In most cases, the more involved they are, the better.

YOUR LIFE AS A TEACHER

Teaching is a giving profession. We give of ourselves mentally, physically, and emotionally, and not only in the classroom—most of us take the stress, joy, and work home with us. We do it because we want to improve the lives of young people and help build a positive future for them. And we get a ton in return for this commitment.

But many new teachers forget that in order to give 100 percent on the job, they must take care of themselves. How do you do the job and enjoy your life? You want to enter the classroom with a smile on your face, not a scowl from being overworked, tired, and annoyed. The chapters in this section tell you how to avoid getting burned out and how to stay healthy and happy inside—and outside—the classroom.

Chapter

NINE

Managing the Workload

How do you balance this exciting, challenging, all-consuming crazy career with the rest of your life? Teaching can be overwhelming. It can creep into every open corner of your life, even taking over aspects you thought you'd carefully saved for yourself. Many incredible teachers dedicate every breathing moment to the job; that's the choice they make and they thrive on it. But plenty of equally excellent teachers keep their teaching life separate from their personal life (at least for the most part). It's up to you to decide how you want to use your own time.

> One afternoon after school, I overheard a group of new teachers down the hall. One of them said, "How am I going to do this job? I don't even know what I'm doing!" She didn't notice the principal, casually leaning in the doorjamb of her classroom, but she did hear him say, "One day at a time. That's how we start. One day at a time." The rookie sighed in relief. "That's good to hear," she said.

During the first years of teaching, the job can be especially all-consuming. It has so many moving parts: students, parents, principals, colleagues, field trips, staff training, keeping up with the most recent research, and more. It can feel like you're drowning with no shore in sight. And it may soon seem like your life has been taken over. The tips in this chapter (and the entire book for that matter!) will help you manage your workload so you have enough energy to do something for yourself after the school day ends—and be ready to come back and do it all again the next day.

LEAVE IT AT SCHOOL!

Do everything in your power to leave your schoolwork at school, where it belongs, even if it means staying late some nights to finish up prep work. If you have a family, a long commute, or other circumstances that make it difficult to stay late, then you might have to take work home with you, and that's understandable. As much as you can, though, do your best to leave it in your classroom. When you're home, that's your time to refuel your physical, intellectual, and emotional energy. Doing so will help prevent you from burning out.

If you want to leave your work at school, you must be efficient while you're there. Schools are naturally social places, and walking down the hall to chat with a friend for a few minutes can easily turn into an hour of conversation. Strolling the halls to gaze at other classes' bulletin boards can be valuable, unless you're trying to plan for next week's math lessons. Figure out what you're going to work on and when. Write it in your lesson plan book. For example, if you have report cards due, then schedule yourself to write five each day while not shirking your other teaching duties. As with any type of work, time flies. Don't get me wrong—I love to talk with fellow staff members. But I know if I let it go on too long I'll be at school until midnight!

One way to keep schoolwork at school is to use a chunk of your lunch period to get it done. Just be sure to eat your lunch, too. Bringing your lunch every day will save you time from having to go out and buy it. On the other hand, if you're feeling burned out or just need a break, lunchtime can be a nice (but very short) respite from schoolwork. Be aware of which you need more—the time or the break. If you need a few moments of fresh air, take it.

Sometimes you must bring work home. You had a doctor's appointment, you didn't have time to finish your prep because of a staff meeting or parent-teacher conference right at dismissal, or you just could not find the time to complete all those report cards. It happens, so choose one area of your home to store school-related material. Don't let it be strewn across your living space. A small box, or a shelf in a closet or a cabinet, will help keep it organized and in check.

BTW: Are you an early morning person or an afternoon person? Choose a time that works for you to put in extra hours prepping and working (at school!), and commit to it. Or is there a certain day or two when you can go to school early and stay late? (Be sure to know what time the school building opens and closes.)

ONE WEEK AHEAD: LESSON PLANNING

Being unprepared is a problem, but being overplanned can be one, too. It's easy to become bogged down by lesson planning, spending hours planning a few weeks or months in advance. It might seem like a smart idea to write out your entire year from the get-go, but that can backfire because on a day-to-day basis, things will change. By the time you get to a certain week, you might be behind or ahead of schedule, or something might have happened that forces you to change how you teach something. When that happens, all of your hard work will have to be redone.

Instead, limit your planning to one or two weeks ahead. If assessments and goals are a few weeks out, go ahead and put them in your lesson plan book as objectives you'd like to achieve, but don't plan detailed daily lesson plans. Otherwise, you'll end up planning the school year twice—once when you worked ahead, and once when you actually go through it.

Use the curriculum guides. These resources will help you understand timing, which is one of the many important things to learn your first year of teaching. Get as much information as you can from the guides and from other teachers on how they're used. After a while, you'll begin to internalize the standards your students are expected to learn at your grade level. You'll also develop a sense of when to introduce concepts and vocabulary, as well as how, and how often, to loop back to refresh, review, and build mastery.

BTW: Field trips are one thing that must be planned well in advance. Do your best to estimate when your class will be ready and when you'll have taught enough of the curriculum for the kids to understand the meaning of the planned excursion. If you go early in a unit, the trip can be used to introduce the topic. If you go late, the trip can serve as a review. Time everything as best as you can. You may not get it exactly right every time, but it remains true that if you don't book a field trip in advance, you won't go on any.

Speak with other teachers in your grade level about how they use specific curriculum. For example, depending upon the needs of your students, you may find that it's better to teach certain lessons out of order. See what has worked for your colleagues.

One final note on planning ahead: There will be times when you finish everything you planned and need a quick activity to fill in a transition period, such as before lunch. Plan a few and have them ready to go: a book of poems to read; a 20 Questions game to play; a math game to play; a book of Mad Libs to do—the list goes on. You can also use them when your class is waiting for a bus or for a performance to start.

BTW: Even though you're only planning a week or two in advance, read through the entire year's curriculum so you know where you're going. When one of your students asks, "Why are we doing this?" you'll be able to explain it clearly and give a sneak preview of what is coming in the next months. Some teachers say they stay just one chapter ahead of where the class is, but that's never a good idea.

UNDER THE MAGNIFYING GLASS: HOW TO HAVE AN AWESOME OBSERVATION

At some point early in your career, you'll be observed. Casual drop-ins can be commonplace, from your principal to visiting district officials, and you can't do much about them. Just continue on teaching.

Formal observation is different. Most people hate being observed, but it's an important part of the job. Keep in mind that the person observing you cares (or someone somewhere cares) about what and how you're teaching, which is good for both you and your students. No one wants to teach in a bubble. Receiving feedback will only make you better, whether you agree with all the comments you get or not.

How do you prepare? You'll usually know about the upcoming observation, so don't be afraid to juggle your lesson plan so you're teaching something you like and feel comfortable with on that day.

Here are a few other things you can do:

Let Your Class Know

Inform your students that visitors are coming to class and that they shouldn't do anything they don't normally do. They can treat the visitors like any adult who comes in, either by engaging or ignoring them.

> One principal would walk around the classroom during observations, asking students what they were doing and why. It was a great exercise to ensure that my students were involved in the curriculum. I would sometimes do it on my own.

Display the Schedule and Lesson Plans

Have your plan for the day written up somewhere in the room, with the individual lesson plans written out, including the goals, objectives, and evaluative method or assessment you plan to use. Include any materials you're incorporating, and if you're using a specific curriculum, refer to it. Remember that districts and even schools have different requirements. Find out what you need to have ready.

BTW: Modifying the lessons of a curriculum you're following to fit the needs of your students is smart to do, but be prepared to explain what you're doing and, most importantly, why.

Have All Materials Ready

In a way, teaching should be considered one of the performing arts. Everything must be prepared before the show starts! Do not leave anything for the last minute. Have all of your materials, such as copies, manipulatives, charts, files for the interactive whiteboard, or videos well organized and ready to go (as you should every day).

Know Why You're Doing What You're Doing

You may be questioned after, or even during, your lesson about why you're teaching this specific lesson now. Be prepared to show what you taught before this lesson and what you will teach next, even if it is from a preset curriculum. You want to be able to show that you understand the role of the lesson in the larger scope of the curriculum.

BTW: Have a seat for the observer already picked out where the person won't be in the way. All parts of the lesson should be visible from this vantage point. You might want to consider seating the observer away from students who are more challenging. They might walk around the room on their own, but at least to begin, encourage them to sit someplace that works for you.

Differentiate

Prepare a lesson that is differentiated so it's digestible for all of your class (see page 51 about using student assessment to help you differentiate). Otherwise, it'll fly over the head of some students while for others it might have been so easy they could have taught it themselves. The observer will see this as a lack of preparation and ability to address the needs of your class.

Be Ready with Past Work

Observers may ask to see work samples that show how particular students have improved, or they may inquire why you're differentiating a lesson for certain students. Reach into your file cabinet and presto: You have samples of classroom work that show why certain students need assistance. They'll be impressed by your preparation and you'll feel very confident.

Be Yourself

Don't fret over trying to be a perfect, award-winning teacher who does everything right. One of the biggest compliments you can receive from your principal or another observer is that you're genuine. Kids feel it, and adults do, too. When being observed, do your best, but don't do anything you wouldn't normally do. Be clear and take your time. Just like it's a bad idea to run a race with brand new shoes, it's also a bad idea to try out something completely new and different when being observed. If you teach like you normally teach, you might receive some valuable advice that will help you in the long run.

BTW: Obviously, if it's your first year teaching, the lesson might be new to you. Even so, try to keep it within your realm of comfort. Don't make it boring, but don't go over your head trying to impress the observer either.

Start—and End—with a Bang

The beginning of your lesson is important, and that's usually the strongest part of the lesson, but the ending is key as well. Most teachers lead in with a lesson, then do an activity, and when it seems that most kids are done, they transition to something else. No! After the activity, bring the class back together, even if you were teaching the same subject in multiple small group lessons, to review and recap what you taught. Then transition to the next activity. It creates an ending to the lesson and a smooth transition into something else. This is also a natural time to clean up and then recap what you just did. See what they learned?

Have your follow-up lesson planned, as well as strategies for helping those students who struggled. If you have homework attached to the lesson, have it ready to introduce to the kids now, so they know it is part of the lesson they just received.

Manage Your Time

Figure out how much time you need for each part of the lesson, and do your best to stick to those limits. If you're giving the kids 15 minutes to work on a part of the lesson, then set a timer for 15 minutes—and give them a five-minute warning. If a lesson planned for 45 minutes goes on for 90, your observer is going to think you're not getting to everything you need to teach during the day. If you plan it all out, you should be fine. Going over your time by 10 minutes is fine. But going over by 20 or more— not fine.

> My principal observed me for about 45 minutes, then said she'd return during lunch to talk. That made me very nervous. When we sat down at lunch, she could tell. She said, "If an observer comes into your classroom and doesn't provide you with feedback, then the person

isn't doing his or her job. Your lesson was great, but there's always room for improvement." I always ask for feedback from observers, whether they want to give it or not. I want to take advantage of the time someone spends watching me teach.

CURRICULUM AND BEHAVIOR

You can't have one without the other. If you have a terrific curriculum planned, but no management of your class, no one will learn anything. If you have masterful control of your class but boring or poorly planned lessons, why would the students pay attention anyway? One actually helps the other.

Implement your management systems during the first weeks, before you take any serious bites out of the curriculum. (See Chapter 4 for tips about classroom management systems.) Your instruction during that time can revolve around assessing your students and reviewing concepts from previous years. That way you can focus on getting your students accustomed to your systems and the rhythm you want to create in the classroom. After you feel you have begun to achieve a system of management that is functioning in the class, dig into the curriculum. Starting your math curriculum on day two of the school year is asking for a disaster. You'll just have to teach that lesson again later.

My first year teaching, I dove into the math curriculum without assessing the math abilities of my class or bothering to set up any management systems. After introducing the first lesson, I realized that I hadn't even discussed how to work as a group, where the pencils were, or any of the guidelines that I expected them to follow. These kids were lost and laughing, knowing it was my first year of teaching. I was lucky they were being kind, at least at that moment. I retaught that same lesson two weeks later.

BTW: Read out loud to the class a lot throughout the year, but especially at the beginning of the year. This is a good way to develop the social behaviors you'd like your students to learn, such as listening politely, sitting quietly for extended periods of time, and raising a hand to share. Read-alouds also provide your students with topics for writing that you can use as beginning-of-the-year assessments and enhancements to your curriculum.

Frequently reassess what is and isn't working with either curriculum or behavior, and adapt as the year continues. The following year, it might be entirely different. You'll always be tweaking these two aspects of your teaching. That's what keeps us teachers on our toes. No sleeping allowed!

DELEGATE: GET HELP!

You might be on your own in your classroom for the majority of the day, but you cannot do this job alone. Fortunately, plenty of people are around who can help you out.

Planning with a colleague is a way to delegate responsibilities to each other. (Twice the brain, half the work.) For example, I prepared a geography lesson and my colleague prepared a math lesson. Then we each had two lessons to teach after preparing only one. This kind of collaboration makes planning much easier, and you'll improve your own skills by learning from another teacher (see page 35 for ways to steal ideas).

Parents can be a huge help, too. Enlist parent volunteers to help organize the phone tree or class roster, aid with in-class projects, make phone calls about field trips, and help coordinate fundraisers. If they have time, the majority of parents want to help. Involve them and take a load off of your back. (See page 200 for more about working with parent volunteers.)

If you're doing a complicated in-class project and no parent volunteers are available, see if a few of your friends who you trust are willing to help out.

KEEP YOUR PERSPECTIVE

A teacher's workload is notoriously heavy, so much so that it can seep into all parts of your life. It's a big reason why so many teachers burn out after just a couple years. But if you implement systems to manage it, you'll find yourself reenergized and inspired each morning you open the classroom door, ready to go.

Chapter

TEN

Balancing Your Responsibilities

Many teachers end up taking on job-related responsibilities that extend far beyond the classroom, which, though admirable, can burn you out. Are you going to attend every birthday party to which you're invited? Help every kid after school? Walk each kid home? You can try, but the more you take on, the more your energy is diverted from where it should be focused: teaching. If you're spending so much time at school that you're considering buying a Murphy bed for your classroom supply closet, it's probably time to reevaluate.

A new teacher I knew began helping one or two kids with their homework after school. Then it turned into three or four, then more. Before she knew it, her school day had been extended by almost two hours. As caring as her action was, it created another job. By the time students left, she was exhausted and didn't have the usual energy to prepare for the following day or week. After three months, I saw her in the hallway, leaving school relatively early for her. "Short day for you?" I asked. "I can't do it anymore," she confessed. "I was falling behind with planning and was just too tired when I got home to even

> watch a movie or find a moment to relax. Now I'm just helping a few students once a week. I helped the rest find a free after-school homework service."

Wanting to do more for your students is obviously admirable, but it can be a slippery slope. There are a lot reasons to teach, and for many of us a big reason is that we want to make a difference in the lives of children. It's a joy and an honor to play such a meaningful role in our students' lives. But by overextending ourselves, are we doing them a service or a disservice? During my career, I have walked kids home, bought them lunch, and helped them with homework, and I don't regret any of it. However, if I ended up doing these extra things every day, I might. Think carefully about where you draw the line.

> I wanted to find a time to help a smaller group of students with their math and provide some extra work time for students who had extra-busy after-school schedules, long commutes, or no one at home to help them. I remembered how in high school my math teachers had started something called "Math Café" during lunch. If you needed help or wanted to get a jump-start on your homework, you could bring your lunch and get to work. I teamed up with a grade-level colleague and did the same thing. Once or twice a week, I would have lunch with a group of students (always fun) and then we would work together on math. Some kids came to get ahead on their homework, others came to catch up, and some came to help other kids in class. I didn't mind giving up my lunch period a day or two a week, and it helped the kids a lot. And it didn't burn me out.

THE JOBS NOT INCLUDED IN YOUR JOB DESCRIPTION

On any given day, you may feel like—or be called on to perform—the job of a:

- social worker
- therapist
- nurse
- friend
- parent

The line between "teacher" and any one of these roles can and will become blurred. You'll probably end up being all of these, and many others, in one form or another. Be careful about letting the line get *too* blurry. If you feel like a social worker, refer to the actual social worker in your building. If you're giving out Band-Aids, that's one thing, but for any medical situation more serious than that, get the real nurse. And although you might feel close to your students, remember that your *friends* are people you meet after school is out, and you are not their mom or dad (although if I had a dollar for how many times I've been called "Dad" by a student, I'd own every sports franchise in the Americas).

You'll already be doing a *lot* for your students, so it's important to do your best to stick to what you feel comfortable taking on. You'd be surprised how overwhelmed you can get. Stay focused upon the job at hand: teaching.

THE POSITIVE INFLUENCE: YOUR EXCITING LIFE

Most people in other professions don't emotionally take their work home like teachers do. The faces and voices of our students; the terrific, inspiring, thought-provoking, or terrifying things they say; their difficult and wonderful lives—all will become etched in your mind and your heart. For most people, teaching requires an emotional buy-in to complete it with care, desire, and dedication.

Because teaching is such a personal profession, many of your thoughts during the day and evening—and even your dreams—will revolve around your life in the classroom. The best way I know to make sure you get mental and emotional breaks from the work is to have an active life outside of the classroom. Go out at night, read the paper, go to the movies, take classes, work out, run marathons, or study new languages. Staying active will keep you refreshed. In some cases, it can inspire you to be a better teacher. It's helped me tremendously throughout my career.

> **BTW:** Invite a friend who has a captivating hobby or interest to class to speak. The kids will love meeting a friend of yours, and it's fun to mix the two worlds.

It can even help to let your personal life seep into the classroom a little bit. Telling your students that you knit, dance, cook, or have some other interest or hobby can make you a more multidimensional and interesting person to them, which might get them to pay extra attention. Your pastime might even eventually connect to the curriculum or a class project.

A colleague of mine was a champion Ultimate Frisbee player. She traveled the world when she was younger, playing throughout the United States, Europe, and South America. She never told her students. One spring afternoon she took her fifth-grade class to the park for an afternoon break after testing was over. She brought a mix of sports equipment, including a Frisbee. Everyone was playing when she threw one of her students the Frisbee perfectly from about 100 yards away. The entire class was silenced. They looked at her and several asked her how she knew how to do that. Long story short, she used Frisbees later in the year to enhance her math curriculum, utilized her tours of the world as a part of geography, and taught everyone how to

throw a Frisbee. Imagine if she hadn't shared that! The kids would have missed out learning about their teacher as a fascinating and multidimensional person, someone they could brag about—and all of that came from a simple sport she loved and shared one afternoon.

The other side of the coin is revealing too much of yourself. I'm always careful not to reveal my spiritual or political beliefs to my students, for example, because I want students to think for themselves and develop their own opinions. And I don't recommend talking *too* much about your personal life. It's important to maintain a professional relationship in which kids not only trust you and like you but also respect you as an important authority figure.

Finding this balance between sharing some of yourself but not too much requires a lot of self-awareness and a deliberate approach. As we all know, being natural involves the confidence to relax and let your personality show. This can be more challenging than you think in front of a group of kids. And sometimes, like in situations where you want your students to develop their own critical thoughts, you need to simply be seen as the teacher and help facilitate their exploration.

THE WELL-RESTED TEACHER VS. THE EXHAUSTED TEACHER

Living a full life doesn't mean staying out every night until 4:00 a.m. and dragging yourself to school in the same clothes you've been wearing for the past two days. Your outside-of-school activities can enhance your life and the way you do your job, but you don't have the luxury that people in some other professions do of showing up to work late or nodding off at your desk.

I was getting a burning sensation in my ear, like I had some sort of infection. I swam three times a week and surfed on weekends, so I figured that was the cause. The pain was affecting my work because it hurt to speak and swallow. I was also getting brusque with my students, and they were beginning to comment that I seemed "grumpy" and that my "Patience Cup was always empty." An ear, nose, and throat specialist checked out my ears and said everything was fine except for one thing. "How many hours do you sleep at night?" he wanted to know. I told him that I was averaging between five and six hours a night. "You're developing acid reflux because your body isn't resting enough and all the activity is wearing you down. The ear canal is connected to that part of the body, so that is why you're feeling it there." He suggested I try getting seven hours of sleep a night and see if the burning went away. After two weeks of seven hours per night, I was back to normal. I've kept that up since, whenever I can.

Sometimes you'll feel so beat, all you'll want to do is run out of the building when the kids are dismissed, go home, and get into bed. But being tired is not a worthy excuse to skip preparing for the following day. And in fact, you probably *won't* get a good night's sleep; you'll be up all night worrying what you're going to do in the classroom the next day. When you aren't prepared as a teacher, you're letting down your students and their families. You're letting down yourself, too.

If you're exhausted or burned out, take a moment after the kids are gone to regroup. Try putting your head on a desk for a 10-minute power nap. Do a series of calisthenics, like push-ups or jumping jacks, or take a brisk walk around the building. Do a headstand (if you can) or walk up and down the hallway. Refresh your brain by writing a card to a friend or listening to a podcast or radio program (it will sound different to listen to adults after being surrounded by kids all day). Maybe eat a snack. Find something that gets your blood pumping, and then do what you need to do to prepare for the next day.

You'll share moments of hysterical laughter with colleagues because you all feel delirious from the combination of exhaustion and intensity. Teaching is a tiring, demanding job. I know many teachers who have left school so wiped out they've

BTW: You'll have days when nothing will go right. Don't beat yourself up. It happens, to both new teachers *and* veterans. When it does, take a minute to reflect upon what went well (something must have, even if it was just that you took attendance). Then think about one specific thing you would like to improve upon. Rethink that lesson or moment in your head, think what you would like to do differently, and visualize how you'll handle yourself in the future. This type of practice helps you not only learn from a situation but also feel more confident in the future. Each day we become better teachers. No one learns without making mistakes.

run stop signs on their drive home, left their wallet at the grocery store, or fallen asleep in the elevator. Know your limits. It's important to rest. If you see rings under your eyes, maybe you need to take it easy. If you're well rested, you'll be more alert and focused—and most importantly, more patient.

On a similar note, if you get sick, use those sick days. Sometimes we get tempted to save our sick days and drag ourselves through the day, even though we feel lousy. It's rarely a good idea to do this. You can get even sicker if you don't get rest, you'll wear yourself down over the long haul, and you'll probably get some students and colleagues sick, as well. Stay home and get well! (See page 38 for information about preparing for a sub.)

YOU'RE READY

Whether you're brand new to the game or you've completed a few years, you're now a part of a distinctive club—the intrepid group who understands classroom life. No one else can understand what it's like except those who decide to spend a part of their life dedicated to the education of young people. No other experience is like it.

There is a sixth sense to teaching, knowing how to capture that "teaching moment," being able to feel, in your bones, when you and your class, a small group, or even one student, are experiencing a changed outlook on the world. Whether that occurs when a student learns to read a new word, figures out how to solve a multi-digit addition problem, learns the names of all of the states or provinces in your country, or grasps a personal strategy that will help him learn on his own, it's an honor to be a part of that moment when "the light goes on." When learning is happening, you can feel the world become bigger for both of you.

But teaching is not just about those moments. It's also about cleaning up puke, keeping track of pencils, talking with irate parents, organizing books, being observed, cleaning the class rug, creating bulletin boards, planning lessons and field trips, breaking up fights, teaching your students how to avoid fights in the future, modeling a positive attitude, finding restrooms on field trips, and more. You most likely became a teacher because you want to make a difference, be involved in teachable moments, and spend your days with kids. If you stay organized, take care of the details, plan ahead, and keep your passion intact, you'll be able to focus more of your energy on those reasons.

You'll make plenty of mistakes along the way, just as I have. You'll teach lessons that are as flat as an old bottle of seltzer, you'll create confusion instead of clearing it up, you'll be too strict, or you'll simply screw up. That's okay. Teaching is not about perfection. It's about being present in the moment and working to inspire your students. The teachers who never make mistakes are those who aren't working hard, taking risks, or challenging themselves. To find the potential in yourself, to grow beyond what you thought you could achieve, is hard to do. Sometimes you'll fail and sometimes you'll triumph. But, if you use your failures as ways to learn and improve your teaching, there are no real or lasting mistakes.

What *will* last are your memories of togetherness with your students and the pride you feel about your full and exciting life as a participant in one of the most ancient and essential traditions on the planet: teaching. Enjoy the journey!

Resources

Beyond Discipline: From Compliance to Community by Alfie Kohn (Association for Supervision & Curriculum Development, 2006). Create a classroom of caring by rethinking the notion of discipline and classroom management.

Discovery Education
www.discoveryeducation.com
Excellent videos, worksheets, lesson plans, and other resources in all subjects.

Edutopia
www.edutopia.org
A good resource for everything from curriculum to politics.

English Learners in American Classrooms: 101 Questions, 101 Answers by James Crawford and Stephen Krashen (Scholastic Teaching Resources, 2007). A straightforward discussion of the issues surrounding ELL education, which can be very relevant in all classes, not just bilingual or ESL. Also consider any books by Mimi Met on the topic of language acquisition.

How Children Succeed: Grit, Curiosity, and the Hidden Power of Character by Paul Tough (Houghton Mifflin Harcourt, 2012). A must-read for all new teachers pondering the ideas of how to develop character in students and prepare them for future success, even in the face of adversity.

Math Solutions
www.mathsolutions.com
A professional development website for math instruction that includes videos, lesson plans, and webinars.

PBS Learning Media
www.pbslearningmedia.org
Free classroom and professional development resources from public broadcasting.

The Reading Teacher's Book of Lists: Grades K–12 by Edward B. Fry and Jacqueline E. Kress (Jossey-Bass, 2006). When you need that list of "i-e" words or words that end in "ch," this is your book!

The Skin That We Speak: Thoughts on Language and Culture in the Classroom edited by Lisa Delpit and Joanne Kilgour Dowdy (The New Press, 2008). Essays by educators about how the politics of language affect the classroom and society.

Teacher by Sylvia Ashton-Warner (Touchstone, 1986). First published in 1963, this classic explores methods of creating reading and writing lessons from students' relevant experiences.

Teachers Network
www.teachersnetwork.org
Lesson plans, how-to articles, and more for all kinds for teachers.

Teaching Children to Care: Classroom Management for Ethical and Academic Growth, K–8 by Ruth Sidney Charney (Northeast Foundation for Children, 2002). Terrific in-class tricks to classroom management.

Teaching Tolerance
www.tolerance.org
Run by the Southern Poverty Law Center, this site has many resources for resolving issues of bullying and tolerance in the classroom.

Acknowledgments

This book would not have been possible if Professor Andra Miletta had not invited me to speak to her class of new teachers, which became the impetus for the material in the book. Thank you for your support, Andra.

Thank you to the editors and readers, from proposal to manuscript: Susan Suffes, for your wise advice. Andrea Franks, Jeremy Carr, Matthew Fishbane, Marilyn and Bob Kriegel, Shino Tanikawa, Brad Rose, Chris Beach, Sarah Malarkey, Wesley Tang, Aileen Boyle, Josh Krammes, Cheung Tai, Ted Sykes and Susan Crosby, my own elementary school teacher who remains a friend and an inspiration. Thank you all for your insights, honest feedback, and support.

Thank you to Anne Devlin, my agent, who believed that this was a book.

Thank you to all of the teachers with whom I taught at Mar Vista in Los Angeles, John Muir in San Francisco, and La Escuela Amistad and P.S. 3 in New York City.

To my principals for their leadership and lessons: Dolores Palacio, Virginia Watkins and Cecilia Wambach, Julia Pietro and Miriam Pedraja, and last but not least, Lisa Siegman and Regina Chiou.

To the educators who have influenced me, opened doors, and helped me along the way: Luisa Costa, Joe Rafter, Stephen Thomas, John Littleton, Lois Kortum, Janet Lederman, and Eduardo Eizner.

And to my friends and support system: Allon Azulai; Lauren Barack; Richard Baran; Peter Bosch; Robinson Clark; Elizabeth Colton; Malachi Connolly; John Delaney; Jean Dowd; Lindy Fisher; Ray Franks; Kayla Garaway; Alan Greenstein; Bridgette Jackson; Lindsey Halligan; Steve Herraiz; Raquel Keating; Rob Kimball; Gail Kriegel; Mike Learmonth; Bruce Mack; Elan Masliyah; Barry Mallin; Katinka Matson; Beth McDonald; Tom

McCutcheon; Michael McDevitt; Ben Odell; Mark Perez; Sara Posnick; Jason, Kadie, and Lucia Salfi; Pat Schandler; Adrien Siegfried; Mary Taylor Simeti; Fran Snowise; Tom Tinervin; Stuart Warmflash; Alonzo Williams; Claire Willis; Dave Wish; Christina Wilson.

To the entire team at Free Spirit, especially my editor, Eric Braun, whose thoughtful comments, queries, and general belief and support in this book made rewriting a pleasure. Thank you for being a great collaborator.

To every one of my students, for keeping me on my toes every single day and teaching me more than I ever imagined possible.

And for her 24/7 positive energy, endless stream of thoughtful ideas, encouragement, critical late-night edits, and love, I thank my muse, best friend, and wife, Carlin Greenstein.

Index

A

Absences, handling, 36–37
Activity sheets, 69–70
After-school routines, 45, 47
Alone Table, 9
Appreciation
    importance of showing, 107
    reward systems, 113–115, 120
    for students' work, 123–124
Assessments, 51–53, 189–191, 196

B

Backpacks, 15–16, 163
Back to School Night. *See* Meet the Teacher
    Night
Behavior contracts, 118–119, 122
Behavior modifications (B-Mods), 119–121,
    122
Bulletin boards, 50

C

Calendar of events, 60–61
Class celebrations, 59–60
Class Parent, 160
Classroom guidelines, 110, 111–113, 115–117
Classroom library, 19–23
Class rosters, 44–47
Class website, 151
Clothes
    students', 15–17
    teacher's, 2, 12, 26–28
Cold-calling, 103–104
Committee service, 56
Communications with parents
    class website, 151
    conferences, 191–199
    email, 149–151
    homework folders, 73–74, 153–154
    importance of, 147
    listening to parents, 147–148
    phone, 151–153, 154–155
    report cards, 52–53, 189–191, 196
    sharing bad news, 188–189
    specific notes home, 153–154
    Weekly Note Home, 165–166, 173
    See also Conferences with parents;
        First Day of School Note Home;
        Meet the Teacher Night
Community building, 121, 123
Conferences with parents
    family members attending, 195–196
    report cards and, 196
    schedules, 192–195, 199
    structuring, 196–199
Contact information, 41–42
Control
    behavior contracts, 118–119, 122
    behavior modifications, 119–121, 122
    capturing students' attention, 104–106
    consequences for misbehavior, 115–117
    establishing, 110–113, 215–216
    reward systems, 113–115, 120
    self-confidence and, 109
    during transitions, 106–109, 210
Copies, making, 49–50
Cubby system vs. desks, 95–97
Curriculum guides, 209
Custodian, 30–31
Cyberbullying, 167

D

Daily schedule, 63–64, 66–70
Decorations, 18–19
Desks
    cubby system vs., 95–97
    students', 8–9
    teacher's, 11–13
Donations, 19–20, 101–102

E/F

Email, 149–151
Emergency protocols, 61
Field trips
　costs, 162
　lunch storage, 17
　parent volunteers, 201, 202–203
　permission slips, 48–50, 159, 160–161, 163
　planning, 47–48, 128–129, 209
　traveling tips, 129–132
Fire drills, 61
First Day of School Note Home
　contents, 48–49, 54, 99, 156–164
　· sample, 169–172
Formative assessments, 51
Fundraising, 57–58

G/H

Graduation, 59
Health, 223–225
Holidays, 59
Homework
　assigning, 72–73, 74–75
　collecting, 75–76
　correcting, 76–77
　explaining to parents, 162
　folders, 73–74, 153–154
　returning, 78

I

IEPs (Individualized Education Plans),
　85–89
Independent work, 68–69
Internet use, 43, 91–92

J

Job-related responsibilities
　after-school routines, 45
　balancing, 218–220
　committees, 55–56
　fundraising, 57–58
　lunchtime, 40
　professional development, 57
　taking on extra, 139

L

Lateness, handling, 37
Lesson plans
　book for, 15–16
　collaborating with colleagues, 216
　overview of, 65–66
　planning ahead, 210
　using curriculum guides, 209
Local Walking Permission Slip, 48–49, 160
Lunch boxes, storing, 17
Lunch responsibilities, 40–41

M

Meeting area, 13–14
Meet the Teacher Night
　learning about, 54–55
　preparing for, 179–182, 184
　sample handout, 183
　topics to cover, 184–187
Mentors, 33, 136
Misbehavior, 115–121, 122
Morning drop-off, 44, 46
Morning Meeting, 66–68

N/O

New student, integrating, 83–85
Observations, formal, 210–215
One-on-one teaching, 127

P

Paperwork, organizing, 11, 12
Parents
　befriending, 203–204
　dealing with angry/unhappy, 148–149,
　　178–179, 197
　encouraging involvement of, 175–176
　importance of relationship with,
　　144–146
　visitation policy, 176–178
　as volunteers, 160, 200–203, 216
　See also Communications with
　　parents; Meet the Teacher Night
Parents' Night. *See* Meet the Teacher Night
Pencils, 82–83

Permission slips, 48–50, 159, 160–161, 163
Personal life, 220–222
Phone calls, 151–153, 154–155
Principal
    collaborating with, 137–141
    maintaining contact with, 32, 136–137
    stories about, 134–135
Professional development, 57
PTA/PTO, 55

R
Raising hands, 102–103
Reading aloud to students, 216
Reading logs, 73
Recess responsibilities, 41
Report cards, 52–53, 189–191, 196
Restrooms, using, 35, 39–40
Reusing/recycling, 79–81
Reward systems, 113–115, 120
Room design, 7–10
Rugs, 14, 97
Rules vs. guidelines, 110

S
Schedules, posting, 42–43
Scrap paper bin, 79–81
Search engines, 91
Seat assignments, 97–98
Secretary, 30
Small group teaching, 125–127
Social media, 166–168
Special education, 85–89
Specialists, 87–89
Staff relations
    key personnel, 30–34, 49, 140
    other teachers, 34–35
    personal contact information, 41–42
    specialists, 87–89
    See also Principal
Storage areas
    cubby system vs. desks, 95–97
    lesson plans, 81
    scrap paper, 79–81
    students' work, 70–71
    supplies, 99, 100–101

Student portfolios, 59, 70, 71
Students' families. *See* Parents
Substitute teachers, 38
Summative assessments, 51–52
Supplies
    locating manipulatives, 23–24
    managing, 99–102
    notifying parents of needed/wanted,
        163–164
    pencils, 82–83
    storing, 12, 15

T
Talking hands, 103
Teacher/union representative, 30–31, 140
Technology
    requirements, 43
    social media, 166–168
    using, 89–92
Temperature of room, 9–10
Tissues, 100
Traffic patterns, 7–10
Transitions, 106–109, 210

V
Valuables, safeguarding, 16, 24–25
Visual control
    of door to hall, 14
    importance of, 7
    in meeting area, 13–14
    during one-on-one teaching, 127
Vital Information Sheet, 158–159

W
Walking the halls, 39
Websites, 91–92, 151
Weekly Note Home, 165–166, 173
Whole class teaching, 124–125
Windows, 9
Workload management, 207–210
Worksheets, 69–70

About the Author

Otis Kriegel is a 14-year veteran elementary and middle school teacher, having taught in dual language (Spanish/English), monolingual, and Integrated Co-Teaching (ICT) classrooms. He received his M.S.Ed. in bilingual education from the Bank Street College of Education and is adjunct faculty at the Steinhardt School at New York University. He is a guest lecturer at the Bank Street College and other teacher education programs in New York City. He created the workshop "How to Survive Your First Years Teaching & Have a Life," which was the impetus for this book. An experienced presenter, Kriegel has conducted this workshop and seminars with hundreds of preservice, new, and veteran teachers and continues to present in universities, teacher education programs, and elementary and middle schools. He also has spoken at such conferences as ASCD, Minnesota Elementary Schools Principal's Association Annual Meeting, New York City Charter School Center Annual Conference, and others. He founded the parent advice website The K5 (www.thek5.com) to help parents of elementary school–age children. You can reach him through www.otiskriegel.com and follow him on Twitter @mynameisotis.

Otis lives and works in New York City. He is available for presentations and workshops (in person or via Skype) for preservice and new teachers as well as veterans. Participants in his workshop will learn a battery of practical strategies and tips to help them save time and energy and be more effective in the classroom. He also provides small group classes for new teachers as well as in-school visits to coach teachers in their classrooms. Email speakers@freespirit.com for more information.

More Great Books from Free Spirit

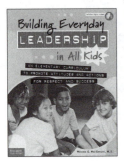

Building Everyday Leadership in All Kids

An Elementary Curriculum to Promote Attitudes and Actions for Respect and Success

by Mariam G. MacGregor, M.S.
176 pp., PB, 8½" x 11".
For teachers and counselors, grades K–6.
Digital content includes customizable reproducibles.

Building Character with True Stories from Nature

by Barbara A. Lewis
176 pp., illust., PB, 8½" x 11".
Grades 2–5.
Digital content includes reproducibles and bonus materials.

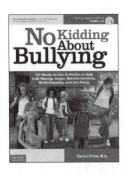

No Kidding About Bullying

125 Ready-to-Use Activities to Help Kids Manage Anger, Resolve Conflicts, Build Empathy, and Get Along

by Naomi Drew, M.A.
296 pp., PB, 8½" x 11".
For teachers and counselors, grades 3–6.
Digital content includes reproducibles and bonus materials.

Make a Splash!

A Kids' Guide to Protecting Our Oceans, Lakes, Rivers & Wetlands

by Cathryn Berger Kaye, M.A., and Philippe Cousteau with EarthEcho International

Includes free online Leader's Guide.
128 pp., full color, PB, 8" x 8". For ages 8–12.

Interested in purchasing multiple quantities and receiving volume discounts?
Contact edsales@freespirit.com or call 1.800.735.7323 and ask for Education Sales.

Many Free Spirit authors are available for speaking engagements, workshops, and keynotes.
Contact speakers@freespirit.com or call 1.800.735.7323.

For pricing information, to place an order, or to request a free catalog, contact:

Free Spirit Publishing Inc.
800.735.7323 • help4kids@freespirit.com • www.freespirit.com